NO MONEY LIMITS
FOR REAL ESTATE INVESTORS

Discover

The Money-Making Secret

In

The Real Estate Game

That Transforms Your

Money Struggles

Into

Financial Abundance

By KALINDA ROSE STEVENSON, Ph.D.

Morgan James Publishing • New York

ISBN: 1-60037-100-0 (Paperback)

Published by:

MORGAN · JAMES
THE ENTREPRENEURIAL PUBLISHER™
www.morganjamespublishing.com

Morgan James Publishing, LLC
1225 Franklin Ave., Ste. 325
Garden City, NY 11530-1693
Toll Free 800-485-4943
www.MorganJamesPublishing.com

Cover and Interior Design by:
Kimberly Lydon Stevenson
kim@spotcolordesign.com

Habitat
for Humanity®
Peninsula
Building Partner

Notice of References to Trademarked Material

Any references, direct or indirect, made to trademarked material within this book have been made in accordance with the Fair Use doctrine as stated in the Copyright Law of the United States of America, Title 17 U.S. Code, Section 107, which reads as follows:

Monopoly® and Mr. Monopoly® are registered trademarks of Hasbro, Inc. Any explicit references in this work to Monopoly or Mr. Monopoly, with or without the registered trademark symbol, are registered trademarks of Hasbro, Inc.

For official Monopoly® game rules, consult the Hasbro Website:
http://www.hasbro.com/common/instruct/monins.pdf

For my granddaughters Kathryn and Rachel.

May you live abundant and joyful lives with "No Money Limits."

ACKNOWLEDGEMENTS

Special thanks to Glenn Dietzel and Paul Jackson for keeping me on track, to Nicky VanValkenburgh for enthusiastic feedback, to David Hancock for his entrepreneurial vision, and Jeanette Barnes, Heather Kirk, and John Roney at Morgan James Publishing for their support. Special thanks to Andrea White for writing the Foreword and making such a difference in so many lives.

Thanks also to those willing to read my book in its earlier versions. Dale Bush, Rodney Johnson, Anne Holmes, Bob Knight, Larry Brown, John Halderman, Vickie Lewis, Mitch Meyerson, Jay Conrad Levinson. Special thanks to Ronda Del Boccio for help with the details.

My most heartfelt thanks to my wonderful daughter-in-law, Kimberly Lydon Stevenson, for designing the book.

And finally, thanks to Jim for being there through all of it.

TESTIMONIALS

"In *No Money Limits For Real Estate Investors*, Kalinda Rose Stevenson tells the truth that nobody wants to hear: that most people who invest in real estate end up losers. Then she tells the truth that everybody needs to hear, but can't learn at real estate seminars. They can learn it in this book, and when they do, they can make the money that has been eluding them all along. I recommend the book and the truth."

Jay Conrad Levinson
The Father of Guerrilla Marketing
Author: "Guerrilla Marketing" Series of Books
Over 14 million sold; Now in 42 Languages
http://www.gmarketing.com
http://www.guerrillamarketingassociation.com

"Kalinda Rose Stevenson has done an extraordinary job of taking the difficult and making it easy to understand and apply—no small task. This book has a lot of heart and wisdom combined into a wonderful read. If you want to take control of your financial future with solid advice, sit back and enjoy this read but have a pencil handy to take some notes and take action. Well done!"

Maria Fee
CEO of REMI KNOX, LLC.
http://www.remiknox.com

"The best way to succeed in life is to create win-win situations. No Money Limits For Real Estate Investors will stretch your mind to see new possibilities and look at real estate in a totally different way. This book will help you develop the knowledge and skills you need. But more importantly, it will guide you to a totally new attitude about money. Using some of the principles that Kalinda covers, I confidently made my first investment in real estate and couldn't be happier...a quick 75% annualized return. Thanks so much, Kalinda!"

Glenn Dietzel

http://www.AwakenTheAuthorWithin.com

"This book is superb! It is a quick read and provided me with many of the missing pieces in my life. Kalinda is a rare talent—wisdom combined with down to earth common sense! I would recommend this book to anyone seeking answers to life's questions!"

Cordially,

Bob Knight

President and CEO

BAK Enterprises INC

"Do not pass GO. Do not collect $200. Instead, take your own money and GO to the bookstore or your computer terminal and order No Money Limits right now. Author Kalinda Rose Stevenson has a writing style that is uniquely her own. She has the ability to see beyond the obvious and draw parallels from—of all things—the Monopoly game. Her keen insights are valuable tools to learn how to build wealth. I urge you to get *No Money Limits* now and don't put it down until you've read every page. Underline, highlight, star—do whatever it takes—to make sure you remember these key wealth-building principles. Kalinda's works are sure to be around for a long, long time. I, for one, am happy to have been introduced to her at the start of her publishing debut. I'll be one of the few who can say, "I knew her when..."

H. Rodney Johnson
Author of *Possessing Your Promised Land – Biblical Principles For Real Estate Acquisition*
Realtor® & Real Estate Coach
http://www.RodneyJohnson.com

"My husband and I invested our time and money on real estate seminars, listening to tapes and CDs, and attending real estate investor club meetings. *No Money Limits For Real Estate Investors* really hit the nail on the head for me. After reading her book, I realize that my money limits and feelings of being stuck were just conditioned thoughts that could be overcome. Now, by changing my perception of money and by being open to creative ideas, I can once again move forward with real estate investing. Thank you Kalinda Rose Stevenson."

Dale Bush
Accountant
West Hills, CA

"I agree that when people remove their blinders and get out of their own way, their limiting beliefs about money will be exchanged for unlimited possibilities of prosperity. A means to that end is the understanding that everything is energy and that our intentions or vibrations and thoughts attract positive or negative energy. Well done Kalinda."

Jackie Cruse
Clear Intentions

"Kalinda's book ends with a challenge. I will never again look at the Monopoly game in the same way. My eyes are opened and I am now aware. I cannot go back to my old way of thinking about money."

Nicky Vanvalkenburgh
Stress Reduction Writer & Researcher
http://www.20minutestolessstress.com/

"If you are ready for a concept that can totally change the way you look at money I suggest you read this book. This book helped open my eyes to a concept not clearly stated in all the seminars and reading that I have done regarding real estate investing."

John Halderman
Design A Life System
http://www.effectivepersonaldevelopmentblog.com

"The best projects I have been on begin and end with an environment that is safe for all to share and network. In *No Money Limits For Real Estate Investors*, Kalinda Rose Stevenson understands this principle and teaches the reader (student) a holistic approach to understanding wealth, prosperity and true abundance. She exposes money myths that are engrained in our society and shows them for what they truly are - scales that cover our eyes. Whether you invest or not this simple treatise provides an easy to understand approach that will help you on your life's journey. An abundant Universe is closer than you know. "

Larry Boehm, PMP
A Project Management Professional internationally certified by the Project Management Institute.
Black and Grey

"This captivating book will illuminate the way you think about both money and real estate. Powerful anecdotes and examples will strategically guide you to a liberating understanding of how money works."

Mitch Meyerson
Author of *Six Keys To Creating The Life You Desire*
http://www.BreakingFree.com

"I've been lucky enough to have known and worked with Kalinda for a couple of years now, and I've got to hand it to her — again!

She's done with *No Money Limits* what she did with her earlier book, *Debt or Alive* —- Only this time she's pulled back the curtain on the world of real estate investing, to show us in simple, easy to understand terms — and using the analogy of our old favorite board game, Monopoly—how our common misunderstandings about money and investing are leading us to the poorhouse.

Reading the book led me to examine some of my most basic concepts about money – and what it means to "make money." The phrase sounds pretty simple, right? But there's actually a lot more to it. And most of us were misinformed – leading us to scarcity thinking, rather than abundance thinking.

No need to hoard it, there really is money enough for everyone, as Kalinda makes abundantly clear. As she says, "Give people money and they will have it for a short time. Teach people how to create money and they will be able to create money for a lifetime."

So if, like me, you've invested in real estate, only to stagger away from the experience financially wounded, and wondering what you did wrong… Or spent a fortune on real estate seminars, tried to do what the real estate gurus told you do, yet still found yourself no closer to making your first deal than you were when you started, don't be too hard on yourself. As you'll discover here, the deck was secretly stacked against you well before you ever walked onto your first property.

It doesn't have to be this way. I urge you to read the book —NOW— so you can learn to drop your old defeatist money habits and experience the wonderful abundance that comes from living with 'No Money Limits'."

Anne L. Holmes, APR
APR, www.boomerpreneur.com and
Coming soon - www.boomeracademy.com

"Kalinda has recognized and clarified the true meaning of making money through real estate. She understands and explains the essence of creative financing like no one else. *No Money Limits* is a must for every real estate investor, from novice to pro. The value of comprehending and appreciating that there are "no money limits" is immeasurable. Kudos to Kalinda!"

Larry D. Brown
Real Estate Investor
Co-author of *Partner For Profits*
Catalyst Equities, Inc.
Reno, NV

"Looking for an infinite return on your investment? Start by investing in Kalinda's book, *No Money Limits For Real Estate Investors*. Kalinda's insightful look into the history of money reveals that the secret every wealthy person knows, that money isn't limited—that, indeed, there is plenty of money. The true limits are the limits we put on ourselves. She reveals why so many good, hard-working people have a hard time making money and reveals that creating true wealth isn't about taking from others, but by practicing abundance. Insightful. Powerful. An enriching read."

Vickie Lewis
Real Estate Investor
Co-author of *Partner For Profits*
Lewis Group, LLC.
Maryland/Washington D.C. Metro Area

No Money Limits! I love this title. It has become my new mantra!

Kalinda Stevenson understands, and more important, respects those of us who want to grow and attain sustainable wealth. She has revealed what I personally feel has been the "missing link" that the "gurus" are not addressing at real estate and investment seminars across the country.

Thank you, Kalinda, for having the courage to tell us the "Truth" that no-one else is addressing. Personally I am sick and tired of the "hype" about real estate investing.

When I first read Kalinda's description of real estate education as the "snake oil of our era," I knew that No Money Limits is directly related to the work I do at Money Tools, Inc.

I'm an entrepreneur and sales person who believes that everyone has the right to understand how money works. I was a coach long before "coaching" became a buzzword. I am passionate about educating people on how money works. This is what Money Tools, Inc is about. I coach and educate my clients to lead their money instead of chasing after money. I dig deep into their psyche to find their talents and gifts—what I call "their hidden assets"—so they can live their lives the way that God intended.

I continually ask my clients this question: "If money wasn't an issue for you, what would you be doing with your time?"

Money Tools is about helping people get clear about their life purpose. When people focus on their talents and life purpose, then the pieces of the "Money puzzle" fall into place and they become clear on how to lead their money. When we become leaders of our life and our finances, more and more abundance flows into our lives.

As soon as my clients become clear about what they really want to do and what they don't want to do, then and only then do the changes occur in their lives, financially, spiritually and physically.

I have always said: "Money does not have a soul, it does not have an opinion and it most certainly is not a family member but we all have a relationship with money."

People CAN change the way they think and act about money and create the wealth and balance they deserve.

One way to do that is by changing the rules and playing a different game. I used to feel proud about how good I was at playing Monopoly, because I changed the rules. Whenever any of us went to "Jail," we didn't give the money back to the bank. We put it in the center of the board, so that we could all use it. I became a winner in the game because I created change. After reading Kalinda's book, I realize that Monopoly is just another scam to keep consumers from learning how to use money as a tool to create the lives they are meant to live.

One of my favorite parts of *No Money Limits For Real Estate Investors* is when Kalinda cautions new investors about rushing out and buying property because real estate gurus tell students to go out and make a deal. She explains very simply that there are risks and expenses involved in buying real estate.

The gurus make it sound so easy. After working with thousands of clients, I have learned that new investors need hand-holding when they get started. I tell my clients: "Act as if you are going to do the investment, but keep your wallet at home." I urge them to get involved with other people who are actually investing and watch what they do. They can practice and walk through all of the steps involved without using their own money, and without taking on mortgages, tenants and unexpected risks they are not ready for.

It's like paper trading on the stock market. People who want to invest can learn what they need to know by watching experienced investors.

No Money Limits is an extraordinary book that reveals the secrets about money that consumers don't know. Take control of your financial future and begin by reading *No Money Limits For Real Estate Investors*.

Andrea White
Money Tools Mentor
CEO of Money Tools, Inc.
http://www.moneytoolsinc.com/

D o you want to know a secret? Here it is: You have the capacity to create all of the money you want. But there is a catch. (You knew there would be a catch, didn't you?) The catch is that you need to know what money is before you can create it. After all, how can you create something if you don't know what it is?

Why don't you know what money is and how to create it? The short answer is that no one has taught you what you need to know. The people who know how to create money have kept that knowledge a secret.

This book reveals secrets about money and real estate investing including:

🏠 The money secrets missing from most real estate seminars.

🏠 The secret in the Monopoly® game that teaches you how to create money.

🏠 The secret that bankers know about using your money to create money.

🏠 The debt secret that the most successful real estate investors know.

🏠 The secret that money is what you believe it is.

In contrast to these secrets, what "everyone knows" about money is that there is not enough money to go around. This belief has been taught around the world, throughout history, for generation after generation. The result is that most human beings live with "Money Limits." "Money Limits" are the direct result of bad teaching.

Your money teachers are not just professional teachers, but anyone who has taught you anything about money. Parents. Grandparents. Friends. Priests and pastors. Television. Books. Movies. Your money teachers are also real estate gurus and financial advisors. Anyone who has ever expressed an opinion to you about money comes under the category of your money teacher.

There are three types of teachers:

- Teachers who know the secrets and refuse to reveal them.

- Teachers who know the secrets and are willing to reveal them, but don't know how to teach.

- Teachers who know the secrets, know how to teach them, and delight in revealing them.

You deserve to know who I am and what qualifies me to write this book about money and real estate investing. I am not qualified by a huge investment portfolio and massive amounts of money in bank accounts. People can have both and not be willing or able to teach the secrets of money. Many people who understand money either refuse or can't tell you what they know about creating money. I am uniquely qualified to write this book because I am the third type of teacher.

My greatest gift as a teacher is my capacity to get beneath the assumptions that "everyone knows" are true. I am a digger after assumptions, a myth buster, a seeker of truth.

Money and real estate investing are two areas filled with assumptions, myths, and lies. These unexamined assumptions, myths, and lies keep most people struggling and unsuccessful. Even the real estate seminars don't dig deeply enough to liberate real estate investing students from bad teaching about money.

I am compelled to teach you what I struggled so hard to figure out on my own, because no teacher ever taught me the money secret that would have made all of the difference in my life.

After years of living with "Money Limits," I finally figured out secrets about money that no one ever taught me directly. This book reveals those secrets. This is the book that would have changed my life in dramatic ways if someone had put it into my hands when I was a young adult buying my first home, or when I was attending my first real estate seminar, or starting my first business as an entrepreneur.

What I have learned the hard way, after years of struggle and study and "doing without," is that there really is a secret about money that transforms money struggles into financial abundance. This is what I want to teach you in this book.

Only someone who is born to teach can understand how much teaching itself is the greatest reward for a teacher. Nothing gave me greater satisfaction in my years as a teacher than recognizing those "Aha! moments" when my students grasped what I wanted to teach them.

My deepest intention is that you read this book and experience many "Aha! moments" and then use those insights to create the life of financial freedom you desire. And after you grasp the implications of the money secret, I encourage you to tell everyone you know.

The reason we live in a world of "Money Limits" and scarcity is because too many of the people who know the money secret want to keep it secret. They keep the secret because they too believe that there is not enough money for everyone to live abundantly.

This book uses the Monopoly® game, with the symbol of rich, old Mr. Monopoly® as a metaphor for what happens when people go through life limited by money. The most ironic truth of all is that Mr. Monopoly limits his own abundance because he is playing a game with "Money Limits."

Mr. Monopoly has it wrong! The more people who know the secret, the more money there will be.

You can play a much better game. You really do have the capacity to create all of the money you want. When you take off the "Money Limits" blindfold, you can play the game of "No Money Limits."

Kalinda Rose Stevenson, Ph.D.

TABLE OF CONTENTS

PART I

Chapter 1

THE MONEY-MAKING SECRET IN THE MONOPOLY GAME

Napoleon Hill begins the Preface of his classic book, *Think and Grow Rich*, by telling the reader that the book reveals "the money-making secret that has created fortunes for hundreds of exceedingly wealthy men." After this provocative tease, he goes on to say that he is not going to make the secret explicit. "The secret to which I refer has been mentioned no fewer than a hundred times throughout this book. It has not been directly named, for it seems to work more successfully when it's merely uncovered and left in sight, where those who are ready and searching for it may pick it up."

I'm beginning this book with my claim that the game of Monopoly also reveals a money-making secret about real estate investing. And just as Hill's secret is "uncovered and left in sight," the real estate money-making secret of the Monopoly game is also "uncovered and left in sight." Unlike Hill in *Think and Grow Rich*, I'm going to reveal the secret. When you grasp the money-making secret of the Monopoly game, you will understand how some investors can create financial freedom with real estate investing while the majority of hopeful real estate investors never make the first deal.

Before revealing the secret itself, let's look at the connection between real estate investing, the hope of financial freedom, and the game of Monopoly.

What Are They Teaching You At Real Estate Seminars?

For a long time, owning your home was the foundation of the American Dream. The New American Dream now includes owning investment real estate. This dream has been fed by a hot real estate market offering historically low mortgage rates and fantastically high property values and appreciation rates. Thousands of people have climbed onto the real estate bandwagon, hoping to ride it to financial freedom.

Just about every real estate guru will tell you that the real reason to invest in real estate is to create financial freedom. What is financial freedom? The gurus tell you that it's the condition in which you have enough money to do what you want, when you want to do it.

The gurus put this promise of financial freedom in the context of a society in which 96% of the population will reach the age of 65 financially unfree. Consider the options.

- Social Security payments, which are not even adequate for subsistence.

- Promised pensions, which may or may not be available as more and more corporations choose restructuring through bankruptcy to erase pension obligations.

- Meager retirement funds, which are vulnerable to stock market downturns.

With such flimsy options, people latch onto the hope that they can create financial freedom through real estate investing.

In many ways, real estate investing is the snake oil of our era. In the Old West, traveling salesmen sold wondrous elixirs guaranteed to solve all health problems. In our era, real estate gurus promise hopeful students that real estate is the solution to all their money problems.

Real estate seminars are big business, promising to reveal to ordinary people the secrets of making a fortune in real estate. Late night infomercials offer info products and seminars. Enterprising seminar leaders sell more seminars, coaching, mentoring, books, DVDs, videos, tapes, and teleseminars. They tell success stories of students and show PowerPoint images of cancelled checks. And the promise is always explicit. With ads proclaiming, "One weekend can make you a millionaire," the gurus promise that anyone can make big money in real estate.

And so with visions of real estate fortunes dancing in their heads, these New American Dreamers spend thousands of dollars buying information on how to make money in real estate. They buy the books. They buy the seminars. They buy the coaching. They buy the mentoring. And they often rack up thousands of dollars on credit cards. The question is: How many actually create fortunes in real estate investing?

Getting hard and fast numbers on success rates is impossible. Clearly, some people do succeed. Some people attend real estate seminars, take the information, and create financial freedom for themselves. The gurus got to be gurus because they have impressive financial success stories. The photocopies of checks prove that some students do make money as a result of the information they learned at seminars.

The dirty little secret of most self-help seminars, including real estate seminars, is that only a tiny percentage of people will achieve the promised results. Years ago, I attended a Jim Rohn seminar. He talked about how only 3% of the people attending his seminars actually make changes in their lives. He attributed this low success rate to "a mystery of the mind." I have no idea where Jim Rohn got the 3% figure. My guess is that it was an estimate on his part to make the point that only a few people succeed and the vast majority will fail.

How can anyone measure the percentage of people who actually achieve financial freedom as a result of a real estate seminar? No one keeps statistics of all seminar attendees at all real estate seminars and their success rates. From anecdotal evidence and my own personal observations, I suspect that most people never make the first deal, much less reach financial freedom or millionaire status.

What can we say about a system of education in which most people fail and only a few succeed? Whether the actual percentage is 3% or 10% or 20%, the rate of failure is abysmal in a system which claims that **anyone** can make money in real estate.

The question is: Why? Why does the richest society in the world produce so many poor people? Why does a capitalistic economic system produce so many people who cannot make enough money to meet their own financial needs? Why does a society that creates so many entrepreneurs and innovators yield 96% of the people who cannot create financial freedom for themselves?

You can say people fail because they are lazy, incompetent, or unwilling to do the work. This is probably true for some people. But what about the people who really do make an effort and don't succeed? What do you say about them?

People who attend seminars are not a random sample of the entire population. These are people who had enough interest in their financial success that they would pay a substantial amount of money to attend a seminar. These are the same people who are able to earn wages and salaries at their jobs. They pay their bills, pay their mortgages, and pay their taxes. They are not all lazy bums.

Why People Don't Learn At Real Estate Seminars

If so many people start out with great hopes and good intentions and cannot succeed, we at least need to consider that the fault might not lie exclusively with the people. Maybe some of the problem lies with the process itself.

One of my favorite movies has a scene between a reluctant music teacher and a physical education coach about a student with no apparent musical ability.

Bill Meister: "You're telling me you can't teach a willing kid like Lou Russ how to bang a drum or something?"

Glenn Holland: "I tried and I can't."

Bill Meister: "Well then, you're a lousy teacher."

"Mr. Holland's Opus"

I'm a former teacher, on the university and graduate school levels. I truly love to teach, and, modesty aside, I think that I'm an exceptionally good teacher. I also had teaching reviews from my students indicating that they also thought I was an exceptional teacher. Teaching has been my calling and my purpose and a source of great joy and personal satisfaction. If I taught a class and only 3% of my students learned enough from my class to be able to do whatever I set out to teach them, I would consider myself a lousy teacher.

As a teacher who has attended more real estate seminars than I can count, I have pondered long and hard on the question: Why do successful real estate investors put on seminars that result in such low success rates for their students? What is missing?

Certainly, students have personal responsibility. If you don't do the work, you won't succeed. But the percentage of successful students is too low to place all of the responsibility on the students. What is it about the process itself that causes so many people to fail?

I don't mean to accuse any real estate gurus of intentionally misleading people. What I do mean, as a teacher, is that there is something wrong with the teaching process itself. Somehow, education got confused with information, and teaching turned into lecturing.

In high schools and universities, students sit passively taking notes, while the "teacher" recites information. Real estate seminars typically follow this lecture model, with the added feature of PowerPoint slides. The experts flip through slide after mind-numbing slide, all intended to teach real estate investing.

I have heard several real estate seminar presenters say how much they love to teach. And I believe they meant it. The problem is, they have no clue how to teach. They say they want to teach people as much as they can and so they race through topic after topic, giving more and more information, in a kind of uncontrolled data dump.

Definition of seminar

And even the meaning of "seminar" got lost somewhere along the way. Consider the primary dictionary definition of a seminar: "A group of advanced students studying under a professor with each doing original research and all exchanging results through reports and discussions."

What goes on in real estate "seminars" is miles away from this fundamental definition.

You have heard the statement: "Those who can, do. Those who can't, teach." The statement is meant as a put-down of teachers. I have my own version of the claim. "Those who can, do. But that doesn't mean they know how to teach."

Define true education

Teaching is not equivalent to giving information. The root meaning of the word "education" comes from the Latin word, *educare*. It means "to lead out of." Education is not a matter of putting information in. The true teacher draws knowledge out of the student. For real teaching to occur, the student needs to be actively involved in the process. *3 elements*

What do students need in real estate seminars that the gurus are not teaching? They don't need more information about making deals, about buying and selling, and finding prospects. They don't need more techniques about lease options, foreclosures, pre-foreclosures, wholesaling, owner carrybacks, and buying with no money down. They don't need more information about marketing and sales.

The missing piece is something much deeper. It's the same reason that most people reach the age of 65 financially unfree. If 96% of us cannot achieve financial freedom after a lifetime of working for money, and if a large percentage of real estate attendees don't achieve financial freedom after spending thousands of dollars on specialized real estate education, something is missing beyond specific techniques for buying and selling real estate. The missing piece in real estate education is also the missing piece in our financial education resulting in the dire statistics.

What They Don't Teach You About Money

It all comes down to money. Real estate seminars promise big money by investing in real estate but they don't teach students what they need to know about money. People want to make money, but they cannot make money until they understand what money is.

This missing piece is:

 Successful real estate investors make money because they know how to make money.

 Unsuccessful real estate investors don't make money because they don't know how to make money.

On the surface of things, you might think that these are completely obvious statements. In logic, they call this kind of statement a tautology. It's like saying an orange is an orange. And you might be saying: "So what? What's your point?"

The point is that there are two different meanings to "make money." One is the "result" and one is the "process." The "result" is that successful real estate investors end up with more money than they had when they started. The "process" refers to how they make more money.

Here's an example to clarify the difference between "result" and "process." You decide that you want a batch of your grandmother's secret recipe cookies. She gave you the recipe, which she never shared with anyone else. So, what do you do? If you want to have the cookies, you have to make the cookies. You gather the ingredients, follow the recipe exactly, and bake the cookies. Now you have the cookies and can store the ones you don't eat hot from the oven in your cookie jar.

This is the difference between result and process. The result is the finished cookies. But to have the result, you first have to go through the process of making the cookies.

I have a very specific definition of "make money" as a process. According to this definition, "making money" is not the same as earning money. It's not just that you get more money. It means that you increase the amount of money in existence. This definition is critical to the money-making secret of Monopoly and I'll have much more to say about it later.

The reason that I am emphasizing the distinction between result and process when it comes to language about money is that people commonly use the language of "making money" when they are actually "earning money." If you earn a salary or wages, you are not really "making money." To "make money," you need to do something to generate more money, not just for yourself, but for the economy as a whole. *ie Microsoft/ Google/a Mentor CDs/Bus*

This money-making distinction is the heart of the matter. According to this definition, Monopoly is not a "money-making game." The winner "earns" more money but does not "make" it.

Page10

And this is the missing piece of most real estate education for beginning investors. The gurus promise the "result" (you'll have more money than you do now), but they do not teach you the "process" (how to create more money.) I have no doubt that the gurus know how to create money. They just don't do a very good job of teaching it to their students.

This is the missing piece in real estate education. You cannot have the "result" without understanding the "process." In other words, **you cannot have financial freedom until you know how to create money.**

The most successful real estate investors know how to create money because they understand that they are playing a game with specific money-making rules. Unsuccessful real estate investors are unsuccessful, precisely because they are playing with a different set of money rules.

What Has Monopoly Taught You About Money?

And this is where the game of Monopoly is significant. At the risk of challenging a much beloved game and cultural icon, I'm going to make the case that the game of Monopoly contains two money games. Each game has a specific set of money rules. One set of money rules is obvious. These are the money rules that teach most of us to lose. The second set of money rules is hidden in plain sight. These are the rules that can teach us how to succeed in real estate investing and achieve financial freedom.

Why focus on Monopoly? Parker Brothers claims that Monopoly is the most popular board game in the world.

If we accept this claim as accurate, the game of Monopoly has influenced generations of Americans and extended its influence around the world. For many of us, Monopoly was our first introduction to money and real estate.

At first, you might think that it's a long leap from a family board game to actual real estate investing. After all, Monopoly is only a board game played with play money. But for many children, Monopoly was our first experience of using money and our first introduction to real estate.

Even though Monopoly's specific rules teach influential lessons about money and real estate, there is something even more powerful about the fact that Monopoly is a game. Monopoly is a persuasive teacher with lifelong impact precisely because it's a game. Players get fully involved in games, because games involve emotions and actions.

Educators claim that students retain:

This is Big

 10 % of what they read.

 20% of what they hear.

 30% of what they see.

 50% of what they see and hear.

 70% of what they say.

 90% of what they say and do.   *How To Learn*

Compare the learning process of the typical real estate seminar with the experience of playing a board game. In the seminar, you sit and listen while a real estate expert, who understands real estate but has no idea how to teach, races through PowerPoint slides filled with numbers, giving you more and more information.

When you play Monopoly, you are actively involved. You draw cards. You roll dice. You move game pieces. You make decisions. You buy and sell properties. You buy and sell houses and hotels. You pay rents and taxes. You use money, even if the money is simply little scraps of play money. You collect money. You pay money. You lose money. You also get emotionally involved in winning or losing.

Which experience teaches you more about money? No matter how many real estate seminars you attend and no matter how many thousands of dollars you invest in real estate education, no seminar experience can come close to the educational power of playing the Monopoly game.

The real question is: What exactly has Monopoly taught us? Beyond the specific rules of the game, Monopoly has taught all of us one fundamental reality. When we play, most of us will lose. And most people who play the real estate investing game will also lose.

In this book, I'm going to make the case that this is not merely coincidence. Monopoly has taught us money rules designed to create more losers than winners. And all the while we are playing this game, which most of us will lose, the true money-making secret is "uncovered and left in sight."

It's the same situation with real estate investing. Too many real estate investors attempt to play the real estate game with Monopoly-like money rules. The secret of success in real estate investing is the same as the money-making secret of Monopoly. It's the secret uncovered and left in sight.

Chapter 2

ARE YOU PLAYING THE WINNER'S GAME OR THE LOSER'S GAME?

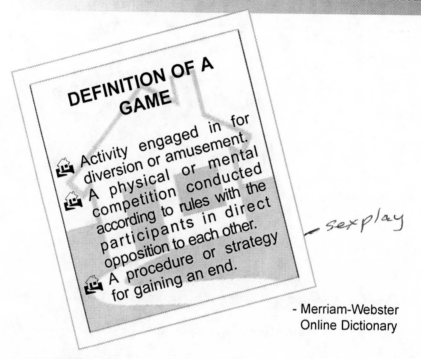

DEFINITION OF A GAME

🏠 Activity engaged in for diversion or amusement.

🏠 A physical or mental competition conducted according to rules with the participants in direct opposition to each other.

🏠 A procedure or strategy for gaining an end.

— sexplay

- Merriam-Webster
Online Dictionary

Monopoly is obviously a game. Parker Brothers identifies it as a "Property Trading Game." Monopoly meets all three definitions of a game.

🏠 It's played for fun.

🏠 It's a competition between players.

🏠 The whole game is a procedure for producing a winner.

THE OBJECT OF THE GAME

Win by driving everyone else out of the game.

The object of the game is evident from the name of the game, "Monopoly." The word, monopoly, comes from the Greek words, *mono*, meaning "one," and *polein*, which means "to sell." The core meaning of monopoly is "exclusive right to sell." Over time, the core meaning was expanded to include any situation in which one entity has exclusive control over something.

In Monopoly, the rules of the game result in the inevitable outcome of the game. One player wins by gaining exclusive control over so much of the real estate and money that no other player can stay in the game.

For many successful investors, real estate investing is also a game. I remember the first time I heard someone talk about real estate as a game.

He kept talking about how much fun he was having. Up to that point, I had bought property only as a homeowner and couldn't imagine how buying and selling real estate could be fun.

People who buy and sell real estate as consumers usually don't talk about how much fun they are having. People buying and selling their own homes are deadly serious, with real money on the line. They worry about price. They worry about financing. They worry about a thousand details.

When does buying and selling real estate stop being deadly serious and start being a game? It all comes down to the attitude of the investor. Investors who see the process as playing a game love the challenge and the competition. They love finding deals. They love making deals. They love seeing potential where others cannot. They love finding money where everyone else cannot. They love solving problems that others cannot solve. I remember one investor who kept talking gleefully about "the smell of money" when he walked into a filthy property with a noxious reek that would repel consumers looking for their own homes.

I belong to a real estate investment club that has an annual December meeting focused on "The Deal of the Year." Several members talk about their best deals with the same excitement as a golfer might talk about a hole-in-one. Then the members vote on which deal deserves the title, "Deal of the Year."

It's obvious from the way the investors talk about these deals that the best deals are not necessarily the ones that make the most money. Instead, there is something exciting about putting together a particular deal that they want to celebrate. Something about the process was fun.

For such investors, real estate investing also meets all three definitions of a game. It's fun. It's a competition. And it's a strategy for accomplishing a goal.

Real estate investors who think they are playing a game know that they can walk away if the deal doesn't suit them. Consumers fall in love with properties and "have to have" them. Successful investors know better than to fall in love with a property. They know that they are playing a game. And if they don't win this time, they'll get another turn.

Playing Games

What is most fascinating about games is that every game has its own rules. At first it might seem that playing according to strict rules contradicts the idea of having fun. But every game and every sport involves

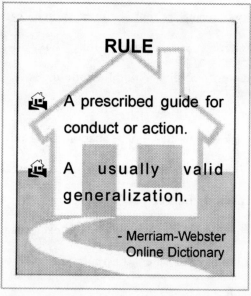

RULE

🏠 A prescribed guide for conduct or action.

🏠 A usually valid generalization.

- Merriam-Webster Online Dictionary

rules. Playing according to the rules is part of the fun of the game. The game stops being fun when people break the rules. A game without rules, when anything goes, is not a game at all.

Everyone who sits down to play Monopoly knows that it's a game and knows that the game has explicit rules. Parker Brothers provides a Rulebook along with the rest of the game equipment. These rules are the authoritative guide for what players can and cannot do.

Unlike Monopoly, real estate investing is an incredibly complex game. No one has written the authoritative rulebook. But even without a rulebook, real estate investing has rules.

- The first challenge in playing the real estate investing game is to recognize the game as a game.

- The second challenge is to figure out the unwritten rules that separate the winners from the losers.

So, Monopoly and real estate investing have three elements in common:

- Both are real estate games.

- Both use money.

- Both create more losers than winners.

Two Games

Now we can take the comparison a step further. Monopoly and real estate investing have something else in common. And this is when we get much closer to the (secret) "uncovered and left in sight." Both Monopoly and real estate investing are games with two games going on simultaneously. The first game is obvious to everyone. The second game is hidden in plain sight.

Monopoly is really two games rolled into one. I'm not referring to short versions of the game suggested in the Rulebook.

The first game is the Player's game, played with Player's Rules. The Players shake the dice, draw "Community Chest" and "Chance" cards, and move their tokens around the game board. The Players collect salaries when they pass "GO," buy and sell properties, buy and sell houses and hotels, pay and collect rent, pay taxes, go to "Jail," mortgage properties, pay interest, and either go bankrupt or win the game. This obvious game plays out to the foregone Monopoly conclusion. One player will win and the rest of the players will lose by going bankrupt.

The other Monopoly game is the Banker's game, played with Banker's Rules. In the terminology of Monopoly, the Bank is not identified as a player. And yet, the Bank is definitely playing a game with very specific rules.

THE BANKER'S GAME

The Banker controls the flow of money.

The first essential distinction between the Player's game and the Banker's concerns winning and losing. All of the Players can lose. The Banker never loses.

THE PLAYER'S GAME

Go bankrupt and the game is over.

THE PLAYER'S GAME

A bankrupt player must turn assets over to the Bank.

THE PLAYER'S GAME

There's only one winner.

How Do You Win?

This raises the question. How does a Player win Monopoly according to Player Rules? Is it a matter of luck? Skill? Strategy?

A Player might win one game and lose the next. When you play with Player's rules, whether you win or lose depends on what cards you draw, the roll of the dice, and who got to Boardwalk and Park Place before you. Whether you win or lose depends on how much money you have. When you don't have enough money to keep playing, you go bankrupt. When you go bankrupt, you lose, and the game is over for you.

But while you have been playing Monopoly following the Player's Rules, the Bank has been playing its own parallel game along with you, a game the Bank cannot lose.

While the Players depend upon luck, skill, and strategy, the Bank doesn't need any of these factors because the Bank has what the Players don't have. The Bank has a different set of rules. According to the rules for the Bank, the Bank can never go bankrupt.

Why is it that the Bank never loses? The Banker can

THE BANKER'S SECRET

When the Banker needs money, The Banker makes money.

do what the Players cannot do. The Banker can create money. The rules are very specific on this point. If the Bank needs money, it makes more money. When the players have no more money, they go bankrupt and they are out of the game.

And this is the secret "uncovered and left in sight" in Monopoly. While the Players win or lose depending on how much money they have, **the Bank never loses because it can create more money whenever it needs more money.**

This fundamental difference between the rules for the Players and the rules for the Banker in Monopoly is the same difference between successful and unsuccessful real estate investors. This is the secret of financial freedom that eludes 96% of the population who play the money game with rules that do not allow them to create money.

And this is the reason why real estate investing holds such promise for investors who understand this secret "uncovered and left in sight." Real estate allows the savvy investor to play the same game the banks play. Quite simply, the most successful real estate investors do what banks do, When they need money, they create money.

1) Be The Banker
Bank

Chapter 3

HOW TO CREATE MONEY WHENEVER YOU NEED IT

What difference would it make in your life if you knew you could create money any time you need it? Imagine your life without the pressures and anxieties of worrying about running out of money at a critical moment.

Contrast that assurance with the uncertainty of never knowing if you'll have enough money when you need it. This is the fear that afflicts people depending on Social Security, pensions, and retirement accounts. They are depending on having money available but they can't count on it. No matter how much money they have set aside, they simply don't know if they will have enough for the future.

What Are "No Money Limits"?

This contrast brings up what I regard as the critical idea of the book: the idea of "money limits." "No Money Limits" does not refer to an unlimited quantity of money. **"No Money Limits" means that you are not limited by money.**

In Monopoly, the Bank plays a game with "No Money Limits." Because of the special rules for the Bank, the Bank cannot run out of money. When the Bank needs money, the Banker can create money.

This is the essential benefit of the Banker's secret "uncovered and left in sight." Notice carefully: **This Banker's advantage has to do with time rather than quantity.** In the game of Monopoly, the Bank has no need to make piles of extra money. The Banker's critical advantage is a matter of timing. Any time the Bank needs money, the Banker can make money.

In contrast, for the Players, Monopoly is a game of "Money Limits." The first limit is money. Every player begins the game with a limited amount of money: exactly $1500. If you are a player, Monopoly limits you to your own money supply. If you don't have the money, you can't buy property. If you don't have the money, you can't pay your rents. No one can help you if you go bankrupt.

For the Players, the limits go beyond the quantity of money. Players are limited by the roll of the dice and the cards they draw. The property available for purchase is limited, even if you have enough money to buy. The game limits the number of houses to 32 and the hotels to 12. Even if you have enough money to buy houses or hotels, you can't buy them if none are available. The most important limit is that Monopoly rules allow only one Player to win.

At root, all of the limits of the Players' Game come back to "Money Limits" and the inability of the Players to create more money at crucial points in the game. The game has rules to punish Players when they are short of money. For example, when a Player needs to sell property to raise money, the Player has to sell at a loss. In contrast, the Bank can do what the Players cannot do. The Bank can make money when it needs money. At those moments when a Player doesn't have enough money, the rules simultaneously punish the Player and reward the Bank.

Monopoly reflects the limiting economic realities of its origin in the Great Depression. The Great Depression was the worst economic era in United States history. It was a time of tremendous suffering and great disparity between the wealthy few and the majority who struggled without enough money. The word "depression" refers to something pushed down. Depression, whether it is economic or psychological, is oppressive and heavy and hard to overcome.

You have heard of looking at the world through rose-colored glasses. Monopoly offers a vision of the world through Depression-colored glasses. Monopoly teaches that there is not enough money to go around. It teaches competition as the only way to win. And it teaches that most people who play the game will lose.

The entire game teaches a limited vision of reality, from limited money, to limited success, limited properties, limited help, and limited options to succeed. Especially significant for real estate investors, this limited vision through Depression-colored glasses is not even an accurate picture of real estate investing. Monopoly limits real estate investing to a single "buy and hold and collect rent" strategy. In every way, real estate investing offers far more options than this.

On every level, the current economic era offers so many more possibilities than Monopoly. Contrast this Depression era vision of reality with a different vision, a vision of abundant possibilities. Imagine the game you could play if you broke out of the constraints of this Depression era real estate game and played a real estate investing game with "No Money Limits."

Money When You Need It

The "No Money Limits" vision begins with a new understanding of money. What is money? Money is not the same as currency. Money is an idea and the amount of money available is only limited by human imagination.

So how does any of this matter to you? The real difference between creating financial freedom and worrying about money is not a matter of the amount of money you have. The real difference is that you know how to make more money when you need it.

Contrast the Banker's advantage in the Monopoly game with the common belief that more money means more financial freedom. As a result of this belief, people think that all they have to do is amass enough money and they will never have to worry about money again.

Too much financial advice focuses on the quantity of money. You can see it with financial planners who claim that you will need retirement accounts of at least two million dollars before you can retire. You can see it with advice to pay off mortgages so that you will have the security of a paid-off home.

The other side of the coin is that people set a benchmark of success according to a specific dollar value and keep striving to make more and more money when making more money is no guarantee of future financial security.

People set out to become millionaires, but discover that being a millionaire is not enough. Millionaires can and do get in trouble when they run short of money. So they set their sights on becoming multimillionaires. But being a multimillionaire is still not enough. So they aim to become billionaires.

The logic is faulty. As long as you relate financial freedom to quantities of money, no amount of money will be enough. You will never have enough money to feel financially free.

The Banker's secret "uncovered and left in sight" will allow you to think about money from a different perspective. Financial freedom is not a matter of having unlimited amounts of money. **Financial freedom is the result of knowing how to create enough money when you need it.**

Know How To create Money

Even more, to live with "No Money Limits" takes away the fear. You don't have to worry that you won't have enough money when you need it. In contrast, when you live with "Money Limits," you never know if you will have enough.

The Difference Between "Money Limits" and "No Money Limits"

This is why it is so important to grasp the essential difference between a "No Money Limits Investor" and a "Money Limits Investor." "No Money Limits Investors know how to do what the Monopoly Banker can do. When they need money, they know how to create money. "Money Limits Investors" don't know this secret and invest in real estate similar to the way that the Players play Monopoly.

Despite this, many "Money Limits Investors" can and do make money in real estate, without knowing this secret. After all, one Player always wins the Monopoly game. Without knowing the "No Money Limits" secret, making money is a matter of luck more often than strategy.

More often however, "Money Limits Investors," and people who want to be investors, run into money limits. They don't know how to make money when they need it. This means they are forced to play the real estate investing game the way the Players play monopoly. They have to depend on using the money they have available or scrape together money by selling assets or borrowing at great cost. And often, they simply can't come up with the money they need when they need it. The result is that they are out of the game.

The primary difference between a "Money Limits Investor" and a "No Money Limits Investor" is timing. Both earn money, spend money, save money, and make money. "No Money Limits Investors" use money with a banker mindset. They can also earn money, spend money, save money, but they have one more critical skill in their money tool belt. They also know how to make money when they need it.

Quantum Money

The next chapter will demonstrate how banks make money. Before that, I want to expand "No Money Limits" even beyond the Banker's money secret to the fantastic reality of quantum physics. I promise that quantum physics is profoundly related to making money in real estate investing.

As a place to begin, I want to describe one of the most intense spiritual experiences of my life. As an undergraduate chemistry major, I was taking a course in physical chemistry. One day, the professor was lecturing about quantum physics and the phenomenon of the "quantum jump."

Before getting to electrons, imagine that you have two water glasses. One is full of water. One is empty. You decide to pour the water from the first glass into the second glass. What happens? No matter how fast you pour the water, the water has to pass between the two glasses. At every fraction of a second, some water would be in the first glass and some in the second glass and some water would be flowing between the two glasses.

It has to be this way because water is a material substance. You can see it, weigh it, touch it, and feel it.

Now let's imagine the same situation again. You have an empty water glass and a full water glass. You decide to pour the water. But this time, every drop from the first glass suddenly materializes in the second glass, and there is never a drop between the two glasses. With water, this type of instantaneous transfer is impossible. However, this is exactly what happens with electrons in the quantum jump.

When physicists first identified components of the atom, they talked about the nucleus at the center of the atom and electrons circling the nucleus in orbits around the nucleus, just as the Earth orbits the Sun. Almost a century ago, physicists studying the atom made some astounding discoveries. They discovered that electrons are not little objects whizzing around the nucleus. When they take on more energy, the electrons suddenly jump to a higher level of energy. What is most amazing is that the electron takes on a charge of energy in a unit, the quantum. This means that the electron is at one orbital level and then suddenly is at a higher orbital level without ever appearing between the two levels. This means that electrons are not matter. Electrons are charges of energy existing as probabilities.

As I listened to this explanation, something about this reality that electrons are energies rather than objects grabbed me. It might seem

How To Create Money Whenever You Need It   33

odd. I was sitting in a college classroom, watching a professor write calculus equations on the blackboard, and I suddenly was overcome by an intuitive grasp of reality that was far greater than anything I had imagined before. It wasn't simply an intellectual experience, but a spiritual one. I put down my pen and sat in dazed awe for the rest of the class period.

I am not the only one who has encountered the quantum reality of our universe who has been stopped in her tracks in wonder. Quantum reality means that the material world we see is simply energy. Underneath the solid matter we can see and touch in our material world, there is only energy and unlimited possibilities.

So what does quantum physics have to do with money and real estate investing? To explain this, let's go back to Monopoly for a moment to consider the most limiting of all of the Monopoly money limits.

Monopoly treats money as real. Yes, I know, Monopoly uses play money. But Monopoly treats the play money as if currency is equivalent to money.

The Monopoly Game provides play money totaling $16,550.00. This play money comes in the form of small colored scraps of paper resembling United States currency. At the end of the game, the amount of play money is still $16,550.00. Although the Banker can add more currency if necessary, the most limiting of all the Monopoly money lessons is that money is the same as currency.

In fact, currency is a symbol for money, not money itself. Money itself is an idea and the currency we hold in our hands is the physical representation of the idea of money.

You might think this is just so much mumbo-jumbo. But before you reject the idea outright, consider what currency represents. Although this is a very complicated topic, the most basic idea is that currencies used to represent some sort of commodity, such as gold or silver. When the government printed out paper money, the paper money represented an equivalent value of gold or silver, stashed away in places like Fort Knox.

All of that changed in 1971, when the Bretton Woods agreement lifted the gold standard. Since then, most currencies in the world are "fiat" currencies. What is a "fiat?" A fiat is a decree by the government. The currency you use is based on nothing more than a government decree that the currency is worth a certain value.

So, what is currency? Currency is a representation of value, based on what the government says it is worth. Do you see that there is nothing behind currency except the idea of value? *yes*

So if currency is simply a declaration of value, and currency is not the same as money, what is money?

definition

Here's a definition of money from the "Committee on Banking and Currency "in the United States House of Representatives, from 1964.

yes Definition of Money

MONEY

Money is anything that people will accept in exchange for goods or services, in the belief that they may, in turn, exchange it, now or later, for other goods or services. Any number of different materials-including paper IOU's-may serve as money. How money functions, and what money represents are its important aspects and not simply what it is made of.

"Money is anything that people will accept in exchange for goods or services, in the belief that they may, in turn, exchange it, now or later, for other goods or services. Any number of different materials—including paper I O U's—may serve as money. How money functions, and what money represents are its important aspects and not simply what it is made of."

This definition is clear enough. You can use anything for money. It is the function that is essential, not the material used to represent the function.

Do you also notice the word "belief?" It really doesn't matter what you use to represent money. **The most critical component of money is belief.** You believe that you will get something of value in return for whatever you use to represent money.

In other words, it doesn't really matter if currency is backed by gold in Fort Knox or created by decree. Money is based on faith that it is worth what you think it is worth.

So, what is money? **Money is an idea based on faith.** When you hand over your paper currency, there is nothing solid behind it. There is only the belief that it is worth what it is.

Let's bring this theory back to Earth. I am making a case that Monopoly is a game with two sets of rules. The first set of rules is for the Players. The second set is for the Banker.

In the Player's game, money is equivalent to a commodity in limited supply. As long as Players are limited to the money available, most will lose the game because they run out of money.

The Banker can do something with money that that Players cannot do. The Banker can create more money. In the next chapter, we'll watch the Banker play the Banker's money game, and see how belief is the essential commodity behind a bank's capacity to create money.

For right now, let's return to the relationship between quantum physics, Monopoly money, and real estate investing. Monopoly is a game that treats money as a material object in limited supply. This limitation violates the essence of the monetary system itself. It also violates quantum reality, which is based on infinite possibilities rather than limitation.

When you grasp the quantum reality of money, you will no longer be limited by the restrictions imposed upon you by ideas that money is a commodity in limited supply. This will transform your real estate investing, from a struggle to invest according to the scarcity of "Money Limits Investor" rules to the abundance of "No Money Limits Investor" rules. All of this will become clearer as you see how banks create money based on belief.

Chapter 4

DISCOVER THE BANK'S MONEY-MAKING SECRET

RULE #1: THE BANKER'S ADVANTAGE

When the Banker runs out of money, the Banker makes more money.

RULE #2: THE PLAYER'S DISADVANTAGE

When the Player runs out of money, the player goes bankrupt and is out of the game.

I began this book by claiming that Monopoly has a secret similar to the "secret uncovered and left in sight" in *Think and Grow Rich*. Monopoly's "secret uncovered and left in sight" is the difference between making money and struggling with money.

In Chapter Two, I identified the secret: the Bank plays the game according to Rule #1. The Bank never goes broke because it can create as much money as it needs whenever it needs more money.

This is a secret worthy of blaring trumpets and brass bands. This is the secret that allows only 4% of the population to create financial freedom. And it has been right in front of you all along, except that you thought it didn't apply to you.

Why You Lose And The Bank Always Wins

In this chapter, I'm going to add an additional piece to the secret. It's not enough to identify why the rich get rich, but to understand why most people don't. This brings us to the other side of the "secret uncovered and left in sight." This is Rule #2. Players go bankrupt when they run out of money.

The difference between the Rule #1 for the Bank and Rule #2 for the Players is the difference between "No Money Limits Investing" and "Money Limits Investing."

If you have any doubt that Monopoly consists of two simultaneous games, these two rules make it clear. Taken together, these two rules are the hologram of Monopoly.

Have you ever seen a hologram? A hologram records images in three dimensions. The first hologram I ever saw was at the Pacific Science Center in Seattle. The hologram was on a pedestal in the middle of the room. When you walked around it, you could see a woman go through the entire sequence of blowing a kiss and winking at you. The information of the whole was contained in any particular view.

From these two rules, lying next to each other on the page, you can see the whole Monopoly game. You can see the end of the game. You can see the difference between "Money Limits" and "No Money Limits." You can see why the Bank never loses and why it is so hard for you to win.

Let's look carefully at this Monopoly hologram to get as much information as possible before moving on to anything else in the game. These two rules contain the essence of what you need to know about making money and what you need to know about why so many people go broke. This is why these two rules have their own chapter. I don't want to muddy the water with anything else.

First, notice the difference in the grammatical subjects of the two rules. Rule #1 refers to Bank in the grammatical third person: "The Bank can never go broke." Rule #2 uses the grammatical second person: "You" are declared bankrupt...

"You" play the game that could end in bankruptcy. "You" do not play the Banker's game. This is one of the reasons that generations of

Monopoly players have not noticed the secret "uncovered and left in sight." The secret is addressed to the Bank. It is not addressed to "You."

It's always good strategy to "begin with the end in mind." Instead of rushing in, let's see how the game ends. The rules make clear that the game is rigged from the outset. No matter what happens, the Bank will never lose. "You" probably will.

And finally, **notice the critical difference that the Bank can make money and "You" can't.** If the bank needs more, it simply makes more by writing on a piece of paper. What happens when you run out of money? Too bad. "You" are broke and the game is over for "You."

Yes, I know. You think that you are competing against the other players. That is one game. But while the Players are doing whatever they can to take money away from each other, so that they can win the game, the Bank plays its own game, a game the Bank cannot lose. And what is most important, the Players need the Bank and the Bank needs the Players.

It's time for a disclaimer: Monopoly is fundamentally a zero sum game, with the game beginning and ending with the same amount of money. In Monopoly, the ability of the Bank to make money is more of an accounting function than a true money-making function. Sometimes, in the course of a game, the Bank runs out of paper money and so it makes more paper money. The way real banks make money is different.

Let's not get distracted with an analysis of the rules of Monopoly. I am using the Monopoly game as a metaphor to make a point, because

Monopoly has been around for so long and so many of us have played it at one time or other in our lives.

The inherent problem with using any type of metaphor or analogy or comparison is that all figures of speech break down at some point. And so I ask that you let Monopoly be a metaphor rather than an exact parallel.

The way the Bank makes money in Monopoly is not the way that real Banks make money. But **the capacity of the Bank to make money, even if it only means adding more play money to the game, is the "secret uncovered and left in sight."**

When you understand how banks create money, you know the secret that sets apart the vast majority of people who never quite figure out money and the tiny percentage who do.

In the classic movie, "The Wizard of Oz," Dorothy and her friends go to see the Wizard, to find the answer to their individual problems. When they finally see behind the curtain, they find a little man, not a powerful wizard. They discover that the solution to their problems is within themselves.

Most of us live our lives scared to death of money. Scared to death that we will run out and the game will be over. Meanwhile, the secret is "uncovered and left in sight." It has been there all along, but we didn't recognize it because the rules said that the money-making rule didn't apply to us. **The secret of creating financial freedom means to learn how to do what the Bank can do.**

What Do Bankers Know About Money?

The difference between "No Money Limits Investors" and "Money Limits Investors" comes down to switching sides in the game. And that doesn't mean that you become a banker, but that you know what bankers know. Bankers know how to make money. The secret of creating financial freedom means you learn to do what the Bank does. You learn to "make" money.

Banks exist to "make" money. The only reason they pay you interest on savings accounts, offer you free checking accounts, offer you mortgages, or any other financial service is because the banks are in the business of making money. The financial services they provide for you are a necessary part of getting you to deposit your money for the bank to make more money for itself.

Consider other manufacturers.

What is the function of a bakery? A bakery exists to bake things. Bakeries use ingredients such as flour and sugar and yeast to make delectable items such as cakes, pies, breads, and cookies.

What is the function of a furniture factory? A furniture factory exists to make furniture. The furniture company uses raw materials such as wood or plastic or metal to make tables, chairs, and beds.

Partial notes To contractors

What is the function of a construction company? A construction company exists to construct buildings. The construction company uses raw materials such as wood and sheetrock and window glass to make houses.

We can all understand how bakeries, furniture companies, and construction companies work, because they start with visible raw materials and produce visible products.

A bank is also a manufacturer. The bank exists to make money. And this is when most of us have no idea how the bank manufactures its product.

What are the raw materials the bank uses? This is where the process gets interesting.

Chapter Three ends with the statement that "banks make money based on belief." In fact, banks only work when their customers trust them. Think about it.

- You deposit your money in the bank based on trust.

- You trust that the bank will keep your money safely and return it to you when you ask for it.

- The bank then turns around and takes your money and loans it to other people, to make profits for the bank.

What you may not realize is that the bank loans out much more money than it holds in reserve. The current Fed rules for banks set the reserve limit at 3-10% of the deposits. If we use the 10% figure, to make the math easy, this means that when you put $1000 into the bank, the bank must keep only $100 of your money on reserve.

Your $1000 becomes $1000 in assets for the bank. The bank is free to loan out $900 of your $1000 to someone else. This is where it gets interesting. The $900 gets added to the bank's original $1000 in assets. But the process does not end there. The bank can now loan out 90% of the $900 to another borrower. So it loans out $810 and keeps $90 on reserve. Now the bank has $810 more in assets. And then it can loan 90% of the $810 to yet another borrower. So it loans out $729 and keeps $81 in reserve.

So, from the initial $1000 deposit, the bank has loaned out $900 + $810 + $729 = $2439. This means that the bank, instead of having your $1000 tucked away in its vault, now has assets of $2439.

In other words, with your original $1000 deposit, the bank has manufactured $1439 and added this amount of money to the money supply. This figure is based on three loans based on the initial $1000 deposit. The process does not end here with three loans. And this $1439 figure does not include interest on the loans.

If this process is not clear to you, go over it again until you grasp the significance of what the bank has done. **This is how banks create money.**

It's also important to grasp how much the whole system depends on trust. If all the people who deposit their money in the bank suddenly show up and demand their money, the bank would run out of money long before they could return their customers' deposits. This is the situation of a run on the bank.

As long as customers trust that their money will be available when they want it, the bank can continue to do what banks do. It can loan out almost all of its customers' deposits, as long as it keeps from 3-10% on reserve.

How Mortgages Make Money

Mortgage lending works exactly the same way, except that mortgages involve bigger numbers. In fact, banks love to make mortgages because mortgages are so profitable. **And what is especially critical to understand, when the bank loans you money for a mortgage, the bank is not loaning its own money.**

I'll have more to say about the differences between Banker rules and Player rules in Monopoly, especially on the topics of debt and equity. Right now, I want to focus on the topic of making money by creating mortgage loans.

Although I am oversimplifying an extraordinarily complex topic, the basic principle is that **mortgages are an important source of new money in our economic system.** The more money banks loan out in the form of mortgages, the more money is added to the money supply. The government then accommodates this increased money supply by printing more currency. The critical point is that the mortgages come before the currency.

And this is one of the fundamental reasons why the Monopoly game is such a poor teacher of what money is and how money is created. With all of the buying and selling of real estate in the game, the money supply itself doesn't change. Yes, the Banker can make more currency if the Bank runs out of money, but this is really an accounting function in the game. This game rule allows the Banker to keep handing out paper play money to the Players, but it is not the same kind of function as a bank increasing the amount of money available through loans. Monopoly begins and ends with the same amount of money.

Trades and Transactions

Parker Brothers accurately calls Monopoly a "property trading game" rather than a "money making game." One of the limitations of Monopoly is that there are almost no money-making transactions in the game.

What is the difference between a "trade" and a "transaction?" For our purposes, a "trade" means that you trade a certain amount of money for something else, without increasing the amount of money in the money supply. In contrast, a "transaction" creates more money, which is another way of saying that there is profit.

A profit does more than add money to your pocket. It increases the amount of money available in the economic system. Here is the dictionary definition of the word, "profit."

definition of Profit

PROFIT

The excess of returns over expenditure in a transaction or series of transactions; especially: the excess of the selling price of goods over their cost.

— Merriam-Webster
Online Dictionary

In Monopoly, almost all of the money exchanges by the Players are trades rather than transactions. The only true transactions involve the "Get Out Of Jail Free" card and sales of unimproved property when Players are free to negotiate prices and create real profit, but these exceptions prove the rule.

When Players exchange money with the Bank, there is no possibility for profit. And when Players buy and sell improved property, which means properties with houses and hotels, they also buy and sell at fixed rates. These are trades rather than transactions, because they do not produce profit and do not increase the money supply.

Everyone starts with a fixed amount of money. At the end of the game, the winner has most of the money. The fixed quantity of paper money gets passed around and the winner ends up with more than anyone else. This means that the winner has simply amassed a greater share of a limited money supply, but has not added to the money supply. The winner has not engaged in transactions to create money or profit.

With only three minor exceptions, every aspect of the game involves shuffling around an existing money supply.

Do you see the significance of this distinction between trades and transactions? **When you understand that money is created in transactions, you will have the secret that will enable you to create unlimited money.** When you understand that money is created by transactions, you know the Banker's secret that will set you apart from the 96% percent of the population that does not know the Banker's secret uncovered and left in sight.

And what is most significant for real estate investors, the process of creating mortgages on real estate transactions is one of the primary money-making transactions in our economic system.

Chapter 5

TWO STEPS
TO FINANCIAL FREEDOM

WHAT YOU SEE IS WHAT YOU GET

F inancial freedom requires both awareness and responsibili-ty. Awareness comes first.

Step One: Awareness

When Napoleon Hill referred to the secret uncovered and left in sight, he was referring to awareness. He claimed that the rich are aware of something that people who struggle from money don't see. When Albert Einstein said, "You cannot solve a problem with the mind that created it," he was also referring to awareness.

The mind you have right now is a mind that is aware of certain realities, certain beliefs, certain ways of being in the world. Your mind has

L O

a certain understanding of money. Until you are aware of the mind that created your money problems, you cannot solve your money problems.

Or, to put the situation another way: What do Flip Wilson, data processing, quantum theory, and metaphysics have in common with awareness?

If you are old enough to remember the Flip Wilson Show from 1970-1974, you probably remember his character, "Geraldine." Geraldine was an in-your-face kind of woman, and her catch-phrase, "What you see is what you get" became part of the contemporary culture.

The phrase itself comes from data processing. The acronym WYSIWYG, (pronounced as *wizz-e-wig*) means that what you see on the screen is what you will see when you print out the document.

You might also say that one of the fundamental concepts of quantum theory is also a matter of "what you see is what you get." Quantum theory refers to the "observer effect." The "observer effect" implies that the physical Universe is the direct result of consciousness. This means that there is no phenomenon until it is observed. In other words, if no one observes it, it doesn't exist.

And one of the fundamental concepts of metaphysics is also a matter of "what you see is what you get." Metaphysics claims that energy follows thought. What you have in your life is a direct result of your awareness.

When you change his language, you can see that Napoleon Hill is also saying that "What you see is what you get." If you don't see the secret

You don't know what you don't know

uncovered and left in sight on the pages of his book, you will not get the result of creating wealth.

Whatever the language, awareness is the prerequisite of change. If you are not aware of a problem, you can't fix it.

While I don't consider myself an old woman, I have lived long enough to see, and be part of, several major cultural shifts. I remember the civil rights movement, the cultural chaos of the Vietnam War era, the rise of feminist consciousness. I remember changing technology, from televisions to computers to the internet. I remember the introduction of Visa and MasterCards, fax machines, VCRs, and ATMs.

I am old enough to remember listening to radio programs because most people didn't have televisions. I saw my first television show, "Howdy Doody," at a birthday party in the second grade. I remember going on a class trip to Washington D.C and encountering Jim Crow first hand when four of my classmates were not allowed to stay in the hotel. I remember not being able to get a job out of college because I was a married woman, in an era when employers were free to say out loud, "We don't hire married women."

When my husband and I bought our first house, the documents listed the owner of the property as "James L. Stevenson." I was identified only as *et ux* ["and wife."]

I remember encountering Deep South racism while teaching in North Little Rock, Arkansas, while my husband served as an officer in the

United States Air Force during the Vietnam War, as the commander of a Titan II Missile site. I remember assassinations and moon landings and riots. I remember all of these things and many more.

Every single one of these social changes involved changed awareness. People saw what they had not seen before, and were unwilling to maintain the status quo after their eyes were opened. It all comes back to consciousness. You cannot change what you cannot see. If you aren't aware of a problem, you can't fix it. But when you see it, you can no longer go on as you were. Something has to change.

This is a book about awareness concerning the Monopoly game, money, and real estate investing.

What Does the Bank Do With Your Money?

I began with the claim that the secret uncovered and left in sight in Monopoly is that the Bank never goes broke, because the Bank can make more money. The rule is obvious, but I suspect that very few Monopoly players have ever been aware of the implications of the rule for their own finances. The reason is that the **vast majority of consumers are simply unaware how banks make money**.

Consider this. You walk into a bank and deposit your money. When you go back to the bank, you expect to withdraw your money. Do you ever wonder what happens to your money in between? You put your money in a savings account and draw interest. Where does that interest come from? You apply for a mortgage and you get the mortgage. Do you have any idea what the bank does to create a mortgage?

What the bank does with your money is similar to checking your bag at the airport. You hand over your baggage, which must be unlocked these days, and see the airport employee put your bag onto a conveyor belt. The bag then disappears behind a curtain into a black hole. When you get to your destination, you wait in the baggage claim area until your bag emerges from another black hole and tumbles down another conveyer belt, where you can retrieve it. Sometimes, if you happen to be sitting in a window seat on the side of the plane with the door to the cargo hold, you can actually see your bag being tossed onto another conveyer belt and disappearing into the space beneath you. But mostly, the process is a mystery, occurring out of sight.

Let's not confuse the issue with problems with theft or having your baggage lost or sent to the wrong airport, or the annoyance that comes when you realize that security personnel have been pawing through your underwear. The question is: How does your baggage get from one place to another?

Probably most travelers don't think very much about what happens to their baggage. As long as it arrives on time, in the right airport, with nothing missing or damaged, it's a matter of out of sight, out of mind.

How is this process different from what happens at the bank? **For most consumers, the money game that bankers play is a secret game**. You deposit money and you take out your money. You write checks and the checks pay your bills. You apply for a mortgage. You fill out mountains of paperwork. If all goes well, you get approved for a mortgage and buy the property. What goes on behind the banker's black hole? Most of us are completely unaware what the banker does with money.

When I first started writing this book, I wasn't aware of the Banker's game. I thought I was going to write a book about how Monopoly teaches players a real estate game that most people will lose because the game teaches such a limited understanding of money. I still think that this is the most damaging lesson of the game. And I continue to think that this Depression era game teaches the wrong lessons about real estate investing, and we would be better off putting the game into museums as a quaint relic of a misguided past rather than into the hands of our children and grandchildren to teach yet another generation how to lose more often than they will win.

For me, the Banker's game really was the secret "uncovered and left in sight," and I didn't see it at first. **The game only hints at the power of banks, but the hint is enough to crack open the Banker's secret. The secret is that the Bank knows how to make money. And what is absolutely critical to understand, the Bank makes money with your money.**

You might think this is just something that happens in Monopoly, but in reality, this is what banks do. Banks exist to create money. The only reason they pay you interest on savings accounts, offer you free checking accounts, offer you mortgages, or any other financial service is because the banks are in the business of making money with your money. The financial services they provide for you are a necessary part of getting you to deposit your money for the bank to make more money for itself.

The first step toward financial freedom is awareness of the Banker's secret "uncovered and left in sight." The Bank makes money when it needs money.

Step Two: Responsibility

After awareness, the next step toward financial freedom is responsibility. **Awareness is a matter of vision. Responsibility is a matter of action.** When you are "responsible," you are "able to respond." Now that you can see the problem, you can choose to do something about it.

In the Monopoly game, the Bank is the hub for all exchanges of money. The Banker distributes the salaries, collects taxes and fines, and is the sole source of mortgages. Players buy and sell property through the Bank. The Bank is also the sole source of houses and hotels. In other words, the Bank is responsible for the money.

In the Monopoly game, it makes sense for one player to handle the money. As a teaching device for the way money actually works in the real world, the central position of the Banker teaches a lesson with lasting consequences. It reinforces the childhood experience that control of money lies outside of you.

On one level, Monopoly does teach responsibility about money. Players handle money throughout the game, making all kinds of money decisions. They buy property, pay rents, and pay taxes. They collect their $200 salaries when they pass GO. They collect rents and bonuses.

Why do Players lose the Monopoly game? They lose when they find themselves in a situation where they don't have enough money to solve an immediate problem.

The critical difference between the Players and the Banker is timing. The Banker can make money whenever it needs more money. The Players have to wait until they pass GO to collect their salaries, or wait until another Player pays rent before they can collect more money.

If a Player has only $150 and lands on Boardwalk, at a time when Boardwalk has one House and a rent of $200, it makes no difference that the Player is only one square from Passing GO and collecting $200 in salary. The Player has to sell assets to raise the money. The rules of Monopoly are brutal when a Player needs to raise money. We'll see just how brutal they are in the chapter on debt.

In other words, the Banker is able to respond to lack of money by making more money. The Player can only respond to lack of money by selling assets at a loss.

What does this lack of responsibility—lack of the ability to respond—teach you as a Monopoly player? The game puts the players in the position of waiting until they pass GO, which is another way of saying that the Players learn to wait until payday.

If you have ever had a money crisis, often the crisis had to do with timing. If you had enough time, you could come up with the money. But the timing is critical. You need to pay a bill before you get your next paycheck. You have to make a down payment on a new property before you sell your house. This puts you in the position of needing money right away that you will have sometime in the future.

What happens when you can't wait until payday? You can get payday loans. You can get cash advances on your expected tax refund. You can get cash advances on your credit cards. All of these are strategies to get money when you don't have money right now but expect to have it later. And all of these solutions carry the kinds of money penalties that Monopoly extracts from Players who need money right away, but have to wait until later to collect it. You will pay high interest for the privilege of getting your money early.

"No Money Limits" Investors Know How To Make Money

Let's return to the critical distinction between the Players and the Banker to remind you that **financial freedom is the capacity to have the money you need when you need it. The critical issue is not the amount of money as much as it is the timing.**

The capacity to make money in response to a need is the difference between "No Money Limits Investors" and "Money Limits Investors." "Money Limits Investors" wait until they have the money before they buy property. "No Money Limits Investors" turn the equation around. If they need money, they create money.

My husband went to a real estate seminar once and heard the presenter say that whenever he needs money, he goes out and buys some property. This is the essence of the banker's secret about money and completely counter-intuitive to people with a consumer mindset about money.

This is the critical skill that sets "No Money Limits Investors" apart from "Money Limits Investors." It is the same skill that sets consumers apart from bankers. It is the ability to respond in a situation of needing money and knowing how to make as much money as you need to solve the problem.

For all of the handling of money that goes on in a Monopoly game, the game does not teach the money skill that makes the difference between "No Money Limits Investor" and "Money Limits Investor": How to make money when you need it. Instead, Monopoly reinforces a sense of helplessness. When you need money, all you can do is wait for payday, find a desperation strategy for generating cash at high cost, or find yourself out of the game. In other words, Monopoly does not teach money responsibility.

Financial freedom requires both awareness and responsibility. The relationship between awareness and responsibility progresses through stages.

Growing awareness can be expressed as the progression from unconsciousness to consciousness. And responsibility can be expressed in the progression from incompetence to competence.

- **Unconsciously Incompetent:** You are unaware of how money is made and so you are unable to make it when you need it. *LO*

- **Consciously Incompetent:** You are aware that other people know how to make money but you know that you don't know how to make it. *LO*

- **Consciously Competent.** You are aware that people make money and you know how they do it.

- **Unconsciously Competent.** You have reached the point where knowing how to make money is second nature so that you are no longer aware that you are doing it.

In the era of the sixties—which I do remember—people with causes were forever trying to "raise consciousness" through marches, protests, sit-ins, and demonstrations. (And yes, many attempted to raise their own consciousness with a little help from their friends—especially pot and LSD.) In other words, activists were attempting to make people aware of what they did not see about racism, the war, sexism, the environment, and any number of other compelling issues.

You might consider what I have done so far as an effort to expand your awareness about money and the connection between your struggles with money and this much beloved board game called Monopoly.

The first step to solving any problem is to be aware. You can't fix a problem if you are not aware you have it. The second step to solving the problem is to be responsible. Now that you can see the problem, you are able to respond to it. *yes I Did Div & no Lease*

In Part I, we looked the difference between "No Money Limits" and "Money Limits." In Part II, we look at specific elements of the Monopoly game and real estate investing: buying and selling real estate; cash flow; debt.

My goal is to expand your awareness from "Money Limits" to "No Money Limits," so that you can take responsibility for creating money as a "No Money Limits Investor," with the ultimate goal that you can create the life of financial freedom you desire.

PART II

Chapter 6

"NO MONEY LIMITS" BUYING

BUYING PROPERTY

Buy And Hold
Strategy

onopoly is a game that requires players to buy property at full price using their own money. This is the essence of "Money Limits Investing." And it also brings into sharp focus the fundamental difference between a consumer and a banker approach to money.

After years of reading financial articles and books addressed to consumers, and comparing that information with what I have learned about money as a business owner and investor, I have a come to a disturbing conclusion. Most of the financial education addressed to consumers reinforces the Monopoly rules for Players.

Buying With Your Own Money

Consider this Monopoly rule for buying property at full price, and paying for it with your own money. The only real difference between the Monopoly rules and much of the financial advice aimed at consumers concerns mortgages. Monopoly Players cannot buy property with mortgages. In the real world, very few consumers can buy properties without mortgages.

This is one of those places where I want to remind you that I am using Monopoly as a metaphor. At this point, the metaphor needs to be stretched a bit. In the next chapter, we'll return to the topic of mortgages. For now, let's focus on the idea of buying using your own money, even if your own money includes taking out a mortgage on the property.

As a model for real estate investing, this model limits you to one of the most difficult ways to create wealth through real estate. It is also the most basic model for beginning real estate investors who think that the fastest way to wealth is to buy property and collect rents. As a financial model for real estate investors, this method increases the odds that most investors will end up the way most Monopoly players end up—without property and broke.

What are the money limits with this model?

🏠 The first money limit is lack of money itself. Many investors have trouble scraping up enough money to buy one property. This strategy of buying with your own money limits you to the amount of money you have available. In order to buy the property, you need to use your own money or take on the liabilities of a mortgage, whether you borrow from a bank, a private lender, or use owner financing. Whatever the source of money, you have to come up with all of the money.

🏠 The second money limit is that this model of real estate investing simply takes the typical consumer method of buying a home and applies it to buying investment property. This includes buying property with conventional bank financing, based on your own financial history and credit scores, and using your own money to fund the down payment and pay the bills.

🏠 The third money limit is the expense of owning investment property. You are liable for insurance, taxes, maintenance, tenant liabilities, and collecting rent even if you own the property free and clear.

This method of buying property with your own money also reinforces the most common piece of financial wisdom directed toward consumers: The way to financial security is to become debt free.

When you buy a property in Monopoly, whatever you spent is no longer available. You have traded money for the deed. This is what happens to your money when you buy property with your own money.

The more money you tie up in a property, the less money you have available for other purposes. While the "Money Limits Investor" is paying off a single mortgage, a "No Money Limits Investor" can use the equity and profit from one property to buy other investment properties.

Having available cash has at least two benefits.

🏠 The first is that you will not be in a situation where you have expenses related to the property that you cannot cover and so end up having to sell the property at a loss.

🏠 The second is that you will have money available for other investments. While you are paying off one property, you cannot use your money to buy other properties.

Compare the money limits in buying investment property with your own money with the possibilities of "No Money Limits Investing." The key idea behind quantum physics is possibility. The quantum perspective on real estate investing is that there are always other possibilities. In Monopoly, the rule that you must buy with your own money is limited and restrictive in its possibilities.

"No Money Limits Investors" know that you can make money in real estate without ever using your own money. They also know that it is often far better to control property than to buy it. *re lease option or option To Purchase*

Creative Financing

The alternative to conventional consumer financing is "creative financing." At this point, I have a confession to make. As a result of various real estate seminars, including a three-day seminar called, "Creative Financing," I have learned many "creative financing" techniques. But I never quite understood what the term meant.

Maybe it was obvious to everyone else in the seminar, but I thought that the word "creative" referred to the techniques until I had the Aha! moment when I realized that "creative" refers to the money. In other words, it's not that the techniques are creative, but that the techniques create money.

Creative financing means learning to think about money the way that bankers think about money. When bankers create money, they are not using their own money. They are using other people's money to make more money. Creative finance means that you use various techniques to create the money to finance the transaction. You do not use your own money.

In reality, there are many possible methods for creating money in real estate without buying property, including assignment of contracts, liens, options, and land trusts. You can also own the "paper" on properties. This means that instead of owning the property, you own the mortgage. You can also be a private investor for other real estate investors.

There are more methods than these. Whether you want to buy real estate or simply control it, you have many more methods available to you than the Monopoly model of buying real estate with your own money, or taking out a mortgage on investment property that places all of the financial liability on you.

Finally, it's important to return to the idea of why you want to invest in real estate. You might love real estate for its own sake and love the idea of owning property.

But if your objective is to create financial freedom, and you decide to use real estate investing as a means to accomplish that goal, the distinction between "Money Limits Investing" and "No Money Limits Investing" will help you be clear about whether to buy or not. Acquiring property is not the goal. Financial freedom is.

Investors will put themselves through enormous heartache and headache to buy property, and forget that buying property is simply a means to an end. If you are really clear about why you are investing in real estate, you will not fall into the trap of buying property for the sake of buying property. As long as you are clear about your objective, you will be much clearer about the various "No Money Limits Investor" options available to you.

Chapter 7

"NO MONEY LIMITS" SELLING

WHAT IS YOUR
SELLING STRATEGY?

HOW TO TURN
EQUITY
INTO PROFIT

DO YOU NEED
THE BANK
TO SELL
YOUR PROPERTY?

Who Is The Monopolist In Monopoly?

I have a question for you. Who is the monopolist in a Monopoly game? Before you answer, remember the definition of the word, "monopoly." Monopoly refers to the "exclusive right to sell." I have no idea if Charles B. Darrow knew the Greek meaning of the word "monopoly." Whether he intended it or not, the name "Monopoly" reveals another clue to the banker's secret "uncovered and left in sight."

What are the selling rules in Monopoly? The rules differentiate between unimproved and improved properties. In the chapter on competition and cooperation, we'll consider selling unimproved properties. Let's focus on selling houses and hotels on improved properties.

When you look at the selling rules in Monopoly, you can see the big difference between the rules for the Banker and the rules for the Players.

Sure, the Players can sell houses and hotels on improved property, but look at what happens. When the Players sell, they take a 50% loss. And who gets the extra 50%? Who else? The Banker gets it. Every time a Player sells a property, the Banker gets more money. In contrast, the Banker can sell anything without a penalty.

The real monopolist in the game is not the Player who wins. The monopolist is the Banker. Why? The Bank has the exclusive right to sell houses and hotels at full value. As a Player, you pay a stiff price for selling your houses and hotels. When you sell, you lose 50% of what you paid.

This little detail is yet another piece of the Banker's secret. The Banker makes money on the sale of houses. The Players lose money on the sale of houses.

In Monopoly, the rule was designed to move the game toward the inevitable outcome of the game. The purpose of the game is to create a clear winner. Players sell houses and hotels because they need the money, usually to pay rent to another player. The practical effect of selling a house or hotel at a loss is that you end up with less money to play the game. Each time you sell a house or hotel, you are that much closer to declaring bankruptcy.

As a teaching tool, this Monopoly rule reinforces one side of the real estate equation. It rewards you for buying and punishes you for selling. In Monopoly, selling is a desperation move. Monopoly does not teach a selling strategy that allows you to make a profit.

Instead, it reinforces the idea that the only way to make money is to "buy and hold." This single strategy limits flexibility, critical thinking, and awareness of other possibilities.

One of the greatest deficiencies of real estate training targeted toward beginners is the emphasis on buying without equal attention to selling. I have heard too many gurus exhorting their students to go out and make a deal. And so people rush out, determined to make a deal—any deal—and end up making bad deals.

An added limitation of the Monopoly selling strategy is that it reinforces the idea that a bank must be in the middle of real estate transactions. It doesn't teach investors how to claim the right of sale for themselves.

How do investors get in trouble in real estate? There are so many reasons why investors lose money when they buy properties. They pay more than the property is worth. They discover expensive problems too late. They over-improve the property. They can't get a tenant. The tenant doesn't pay. The rent doesn't cover the expenses. The list is long. Almost all come back to buying without knowing the costs and having no money-making exit strategy before you buy. Getting into the deal without being clear about getting out of the deal is the shortest path to losing money.

David
Las

Strategic Selling

The best real estate education teaches students at the outset how to think strategically about getting out of the deal before you commit yourself to getting in. In other words, you define your exit strategy before you figure out your buying strategy. To know when you get in, how you will get out, and under what circumstances. And it is worth emphasizing that the selling strategy needs to be profitable.

Monopoly requires a "buy and hold" strategy to win the game. Players must use their own money to buy property. This means they trade money for property. Or to use another term, they now have 100% equity in the property. The practical result is that they no longer have that money available for other purposes. The Player must rely on income from rents as the only source of money from the property.

But notice what happens to the money. The money goes to the Bank. What does the Bank do with the money? It puts the money to work.

This is one more piece of the Banker's secret. **The banks know that the secret of making more money is to keep the money moving.** You can gain much insight into the nature of money by reflecting on why money is called "currency." Money is called currency because it flows and circulates the way water flows in river currents

Imagine you deposit $1000 into the bank. Contrary to the images I had as a child, the bank does not take the money and stick it into a vault somewhere. It keeps the money moving. It keeps loaning the money again and again.

Compare what the bank does with money with the typical financial advice given to consumers. Financial experts advise you: "Save your money." "Lock it up." "Hang onto it."

This is not what the bank does. The bank keeps money moving. When the bank writes a mortgage, it loans you money, but that is not the end of it. It keeps loaning on the same money. Each time, a bit of reserve is kept aside, but most of the money is loaned and reloaned and reloaned. And every time the bank loans money, it makes more money. This is why the bank never runs out of money, but you do.

What happens to money when you save it? In a fundamental sense, it ceases to be money. The money stops moving and when it stops moving, it stops being money.

The reason goes back to the essential nature of money as energy. The definition of energy is the capacity to work. Since money is energy, money is also dynamic and has the capacity to work. When money stops moving, it stops being energy.

Let's consider the concept of equity. You will often hear advice to pay off your mortgage on your home as soon as possible. From one perspective, the arguments make sense. You will own your property free and clear. You no longer have mortgage payments. You will save thousands of dollars in interest expenses. And you will have the psychological security of owning your home.

All of these statements are true. But they ignore a significant fact. Equity is not the same as money. Equity is the difference between the value of the property and whatever debt you have on the property. So, if the market value of your property is $500,000 and you have no debt, your equity is $500,000. On paper, this looks great. The problem is that you cannot spend equity because equity is not money.

Equity also depends on that illusive concept of market value. Market value is what the market will pay for your house. And it doesn't matter what the appraised value of your property is—and appraisals can vary depending on who did the appraising—a property is worth only what someone will pay for it. This means that your $500,000 in equity could shrink dramatically, depending on market conditions and available buyers.

From an energetic perspective, money is energy and equity is potential energy. You can always convert the potential energy of equity back into the energy of money and put the money to work again. How do you do that? You sell the property and collect the money. Or you borrow against it. The hard economic fact is that having one hundred percent equity in your property does you no good until you convert equity to cash.

Real estate investors get excited over the prospect of finding a property with one hundred percent equity owned by a financially distressed seller. Very often, this distressed seller is an elderly person who cannot pay the property tax, cannot pay for repairs, and has no money to handle medical treatments. At the same time, the owner has a paid-off mortgage. The problem is that the owner doesn't know how to convert the equity in the property to money.

This is a situation ripe for an investor to buy the property from the distressed seller, and make a substantial profit. Whether this is fair, legal, or ethical is another matter. From a financial perspective, this situation demonstrates the fundamental problem with trading your money for equity. Until you sell the property or borrow against the equity, no amount of equity is going to pay the bills.

It's also significant to point out that while you are pouring cash into a property, to pay off the mortgage, the bank is playing a different game. The bank does not tie up money in one property, but keeps reinvesting it. The bank keeps making more and more money on the same money. Meanwhile, any money you leave as equity in your property is no longer working and can no longer make money.

The secret "uncovered and left in sight" also applies to selling real estate. Just as there are creative financing techniques, there are also creative selling techniques. The secret is to apply banker knowledge about money to the process of selling.

When you sell a property, you are converting the potential energy of equity into the energy of money. Put another way, it truly doesn't matter how much equity you have in investment properties. Until you sell or borrow against the property, you have not made a profit.

When you do make a profit by selling, you can follow the example of banks and become the bank for the buyer. You can take back mortgage notes on property you sell, and then take your profits and invest in other properties.

The most significant insight from the Banker's game is to keep your money moving so that you can do what the banker does. You can make a profit when you buy and also when you sell.

Keep your money Moving —
ITs The energy

Chapter 8

"NO MONEY LIMITS" CASH FLOW

WHAT IS YOUR
CASH FLOW
STRATEGY?

onopoly allows a single model for Players to win the game. This is the model of buying and holding rental property. Monopoly also imposes rules that make buying and holding real estate in the game even tougher than it was to buy and hold real estate in 1934.

The model also forces the investor to depend on collecting rents as a means to build wealth. Unlike investing in real properties, where you have the possibility of appreciation, in Monopoly, you must depend exclusively on cash flow to increase wealth. And Monopoly even imposes a rule on Players that they cannot collect rent on mortgaged property.

Monopoly and the Great Depression

Before looking more closely at this "buy and hold" strategy in Monopoly, it's essential to set Monopoly in its historical context of the Great Depression. Two relevant events occurred in 1934. The first is that 1934 was the year when Charles B. Darrow introduced the Monopoly game to Parker Brothers.

Darrow was an unemployed engineer living in Germantown, Pennsylvania. In 1933, Darrow found "The Landlord's Game," patented in 1904 by Lizzie Magie. Magie wanted to show how rents enriched property owners and impoverished tenants. Darrow modified "The Landlord's Game" to produce his own game. As the story goes, he played it with his family for his own amusement. As word of the game spread, he began to make and sell his own copies.

Convinced that he had found the secret of creating his own fortune, he attempted to sell the game to Parker Brothers in 1934, but they were not interested, claiming that there were 52 "design errors" in the game. Parker Brothers changed its decision about the game as Darrow's version of the game became more popular. In 1935, Parker Brothers bought the rights to the game from Darrow. Parker Brothers also paid Magie for the rights to the game, so that it could promote Darrow as the inventor of the game. As a result, Parker Brothers paid royalties on all games sold and Darrow became a millionaire.

The essential points I want to emphasize from this brief summary are these:

- Darrow was an unemployed employee who found his own way to riches through the Monopoly Game, not through buying and selling real estate.

- Darrow changed the purpose of the original game. Magie's game was a social commentary about the unfairness of creating wealth through rents, with the result that renters become impoverished. Darrow's game celebrates the creation of wealth through rents, by impoverishing renters.

The other significant event in 1934 was the introduction of a new type of mortgage. In an effort to stimulate the economy in the Great Depression, The Federal Housing Administration (FHA) created mortgages aimed at people who could not get mortgages under existing mortgages programs.

In 1934, 40% of the households owned homes and 60% rented. The only available mortgages set terms that few people could meet. Loans were limited to 50% of the market value and repayment was required within 3 to 5 years, with a balloon payment at the end.

In that economic environment, only a small percentage of the population could afford to buy investment property and collect rent as landlords. The game plays upon the hopes and fears of people who couldn't even buy their own homes, much less become real estate tycoons.

The big changes that the FHA made are changes that all of us now take for granted. The FHA lowered down payment requirements. They offered mortgages with 80 or 90 percent loan-to-value, instead of the existing 50 percent loan-to-value programes of the era. They also introduced longer repayment periods, expanding 3-5 year mortgages to 15-30 year mortgages.

Just in passing, I want to point out that the mortgage rates in Monopoly are 50% of the value of the property, reflecting the mortgage practices of the era, rather than the lower mortgage rates introduced by the FHA in 1934.

The FHA also started the trend of "qualifying" applicants for loans based on their ability to repay the loan. Before that, mortgages were granted based on "knowing people." In other words, what we take for granted as the terms of conventional mortgages did not exist when Monopoly was first introduced. It is also important to note that there is no hint of this new reality in the game of Monopoly.

Darrow's version of Monopoly reflects a harsh economic environment which prevented most people from owning property and caused renters great hardship.

Monopoly would not have endured this long, and become so popular with so many people, if it did not somehow satisfy deep emotional longings.

Put yourself in the position of someone who is unemployed, scraping for money, and has to pay rent to a wealthy landlord. While the landlord gets richer, you get poorer and see no way out.

The Mr. Monopoly caricature captures the essence of the 1934 landlord. Obviously rich, dressed in clothing only the rich would wear, clutching his moneybag, this caricature landlord is a far cry from the clothing, dress and demeanor of people who were down and out in the Great Depression. The Monopoly game allows people to make a fantasy leap into the experience of being Mr. Monopoly.

Psychologically, this game allows tenants to feel what it is like to be the landlord rather than the tenant. Even renters can experience the feeling of collecting rent money and owning real estate, even if the money is only play money and the real estate is simply a spot on a game board.

It also allows players to experience the heady thrill of being the big shot for a change. Or as Edward P. Parker, former president of Parker Brothers put it, the magic of the Monopoly game is "clobbering your best friend without doing any damage."

What is most interesting is that the game of Monopoly reflects neither the social concern of Magie's game nor the new mortgage possibilities introduced by the FHA in 1934. What the game does is give players an opportunity to be the landlord and get rich at the expense of tenants.

Table 1 - Buy and Hold

	A	B	C	D	E	F	G	H
1	Property	Purchase Price	# Props	Prior Houses	Total Invested	Rent	Cash on Cash Return	Break Even
2	Mediterranean Ave.	$60	1	0	$60	$2	3%	30.0
3	1 House	$50	2	0	$170	$10	6%	17.0
4	2 Houses	$50	2	2	$270	$30	11%	9.0
5	3 Houses	$50	2	4	$370	$90	24%	4.1
6	4 Houses	$50	2	6	$470	$160	34%	2.9
7	Hotel	$50	2	8	$570	$250	44%	2.3
8	Baltic Ave.	$60	1	0	$60	$4	7%	15
9	1 House	$50	2	0	$170	$20	12%	8.5
10	2 Houses	$50	2	2	$270	$60	22%	4.5
11	3 Houses	$50	2	4	$370	$180	49%	2.1
12	4 Houses	$50	2	6	$470	$320	68%	1.5
13	Hotel	$50	2	8	$570	$450	79%	1.3
14	Boardwalk	$400	1	0	$400	$50	13%	8.0
15	1 House	$200	2	0	$950	$200	21%	4.8
16	2 Houses	$200	2	2	$1,350	$600	44%	2.3
17	3 Houses	$200	2	4	$1,750	$1,400	80%	1.3
18	4 Houses	$200	2	6	$2,150	$1,700	79%	1.3
19	Hotel	$200	2	8	$2,550	$2,000	78%	1.3
20	Park Place	$350	1	0	$350	$35	10%	10.0
21	1 House	$200	2	0	$950	$175	18%	5.4
22	2 Houses	$200	2	2	$1,350	$500	37%	2.7
23	3 Houses	$200	2	4	$1,750	$1,100	63%	1.6
24	4 Houses	$200	2	6	$2,150	$1,300	60%	1.7
25	Hotel	$200	2	8	$2,550	$2,000	78%	1.3

Key for Table 1

Column A	Property Name and the number of houses.
Column B	Purchase Price of the each piece of property or houses.
Column C	Whether you own one property or 2 properties in the color-group. In order to buy houses, you need to own both properties in the color-group.
Column D	The number of houses you owned before this purchase.
Column E	The sum of the initial property purchase plus each additional house or hotel.
Column F	Rent
Column G	Cash on Cash Return, which determines the cash income on the cash invested, by dividing annual dollar income by total dollar investment. In this case, the percentage is the Total Rent divided by the total invested.
Column H	The Break Even point, which is the number of times a Player must land on the property and pay rent before the owner recoups the cost of buying the property and making improvements.

The Buy and Hold Model

The question is: How realistic is this "buy and hold" strategy as a model for investors? Let's look first at the financial data for two specific Monopoly properties: Mediterranean Avenue and Boardwalk. These are the cheapest and the most expensive of the Monopoly properties with the potential to add houses and hotels.

If you look carefully at these numbers, you can draw two evident conclusions.

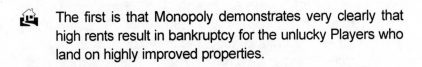 The first is that Monopoly demonstrates very clearly that high rents result in bankruptcy for the unlucky Players who land on highly improved properties.

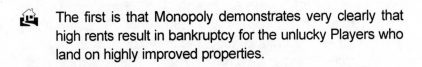 The second is that these numbers are fantastically unrealistic.

Just look at the numbers for Mediterranean Avenue. If a Player owns Mediterranean Avenue and does not own Baltic Avenue, the rent is $2 (Row 2, Column F.) By the time a Player owns both properties and a hotel on Mediterranean Avenue the rent has jumped to $250 (Row 7, Column F.)

With Boardwalk the jump is even steeper. The initial rent for the unimproved property is $50 (Row 14, Column F.) By the time the lucky Player who managed to snatch up both Boardwalk and Park Place puts a hotel on Boardwalk, the rent jumps to a fantastic $2000 (Row 19, Column F.) This is a great way to win the Monopoly game. The question is: What does this method of increasing rents to sky-high levels teach Players about investing in real estate?

Although I don't know the 52 "design errors" Parker Brothers found in its original rejection of the Monopoly Game, I can identify several significant design errors involved in the game when it comes to collecting rents on properties. At this point, I'll remind myself and my readers that my goal is not to do a detailed analysis of the Monopoly game, so I'll limit myself to two specific problems related to real estate investing.

The first is the compounding of rents to absurd levels. As a teaching device, these rents give an unrealistic understanding of how cash flow really works. The total cost of buying Boardwalk, Park Place and putting a hotel on Boardwalk is $2550 (Row 19, Column E.) Rent for the unlucky player who lands on Boardwalk is $2000 (Row 19, Column F.) This is a 78% cash on cash return on investment. In the real world, no one guest pays 78% of the cost of the hotel for a one-night visit, no matter how luxurious the hotel.

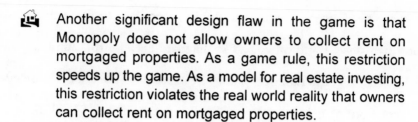 Another significant design flaw in the game is that Monopoly does not allow owners to collect rent on mortgaged properties. As a game rule, this restriction speeds up the game. As a model for real estate investing, this restriction violates the real world reality that owners can collect rent on mortgaged properties.

Let's fast forward to the 21st century, and consider this "buy with your own money and hold to collect rents" model as a method of creating real estate wealth.

The Monopoly model of owning rental property outright has its advantages. You get the benefits of appreciation as the value of your property increases over time. You get monthly cash flow in the form of rents from your tenants. You get tax benefits. You are debt free. With no mortgage, all of the cash flow is yours.

What can we see when we look at this "buy with your own money and hold to collect rents" model from the perspective of the Monopoly Banker's game? While the Players play the Players' game, focusing on buying and selling and collecting rents, with the hope of driving the other Players bankrupt, what is the Banker doing? The Banker never loses sight of the Bank's real function. The Bank keeps track of the money. That is what bankers do.

Getting The Numbers Right

When I was in high school, my mother got a job as a bookkeeper in a bank. I didn't have a clear idea of what she did, except that she sat in a back room of the bank with a group of other low-paid women doing the bookkeeping. Once a month, the bookkeepers had to close the books. More than once, my mother had to stay late because the numbers were off. She said that the numbers had to be exact. If the accounts were even one penny out of balance, everyone had to stay until they found the error. They had to get the numbers right.

If we don't get distracted by analyzing the rules of Monopoly and comparing those rules to real world investing, once again we can learn something from the Banker that can make the difference between "No Money Limits Investing" and "Money Limits Investing."

You might think that "No Money Limits Investors" reach a point where they no longer have to pay attention to money. In fact, paying attention to money is one of the big differences between "No Money Limits Investors" and "Money Limits Investors."

Ask a successful investor about "cash on cash returns" on their residential rentals or "gross rent multipliers" on their commercial properties, and they will know the numbers. Or to put it differently, "No Money Limits Investors" know that they are in business.

What is a business? It doesn't matter what business you are in. If you are in business, your purpose is to make money.

Bankers have a real advantage in business. They never forget that they are in the money business. Since banks exist to make money, banks pay attention to the numbers.

In contrast, people involved in other businesses can get so distracted by doing whatever the business does that they forget that they are in business to make money. Then they think that paying attention to the numbers is a distraction from their business.

I once took a day-long course in San Francisco called, "Accounting for Non-Accountants." This was all part of my own transition from academic to businesswoman. Obviously, a one-day course is not enough to teach much more than a few basic concepts. But I have not forgotten one comment by the teacher. He said that the biggest mistake business owners make is to hand over responsibly for the money to someone else. You can hire people to keep the books, but you really do need to know what is happening with the money.

Let's go back to the example of the bakery. It's so easy to think that the business is about bread and cakes. It's not. The real product of the bakery is money. The breads and cakes are just a means to make money.

This is how investors lose sight of their purpose. When you start to invest in real estate, you are in business. The property is not your business. You are in the business of making money with the property.

It's too easy for beginning investors to get in over their heads with the money. They think that they are in the business of buying real estate, so they buy investment properties without counting the costs. They will buy properties with negative cash flow, hoping that sooner or later, they will get their money back as the properties appreciate in value.

Monopoly teaches Players to buy property with cash, and then depend on rents to build wealth, hoping that you will be the one to put hotels on Boardwalk and Park Place and force the other Players into bankruptcy. The most valuable Banker lesson anyone can learn by playing Monopoly is to forget hoping for such fantastic returns and pay attention to the numbers by counting the costs.

Look at the figures for Mediterranean Avenue. To reach the point in the game where you can put a house on Mediterranean Avenue, you need to spend $170 (Row 3, Column E.)   How much rent can you collect after spending $170? You get $10 each time a player lands on Mediterranean Avenue (Row 3, Column F.)   Look at the break even point (Row 3, Column F.)   Players have to land on that property 17 times for you to break even (Row 3, Column H.)   The cash on cash return for one house on Mediterranean Avenue is 6% (Row 3, Column G.)

Let's not quibble over the details of the game, and the fact that you can add additional houses and collect rents. Monopoly confuses the issue by allowing you to increase rents by adding houses to a single property. This means you can collect more rent from a single Player who lands on Mediterranean Avenue if you add more houses.

In reality, you are not going to do that with a single rental property. Let's keep focused on a real world comparison. You have a rental property with a single house. To keep the numbers simple, let's say you paid $200,000 in cash for the property and can collect $2000 in rent each month. Just for the purposes of doing the math, let's assume that you have no expenses on the property.

How long will it take for you to reach the break even point? $200,000 divided by $2000 equals 100. In other words, you have to collect $2000 each month for 100 months to reach the break even point. 100 months is 8.34 years. This means that you will have to collect rent for 8.34 years before you get back the money you spent on the property. Then you can start making a profit on your investment.

Using the same numbers, what is the "cash on cash return"? "Cash on cash" is the annual dollar income divided by the total dollar investment. $2000 x 12 months = 24,000 divided by 200,000 equals 12%. In other words, your rate of return is 12%

We can get more complicated by adding taxes, insurance, maintenance, and repairs. We can also factor in whether or not you have a mortgage, or whether you put up all the cash. We can also calculate the numbers if the property is vacant or the tenant doesn't pay, but this gets too complicated for my point.

My point is that investing in rental real estate, with a "buy and hold" strategy, is not a get rich quick method. It means that when you learn to play the Banker's game as a "No Money Limits Investor," you count the costs. As an education into cash flow, Players can learn a lot by studying the numbers for Monopoly at the one house level, whether it is Mediterranean Avenue, Boardwalk, or any other Monopoly property. These numbers are more meaningful indicators of cash flow in investment property. You might win Monopoly with a 78% "cash on cash return" but you are not going to make that kind of return with a "buy and hold" strategy on residential real estate.

Chapter 9

"NO MONEY LIMITS" DEBT

CONSUMER DEBT
OR
INVESTOR DEBT?

HOW TO
USE DEBT
TO CREATE WEALTH

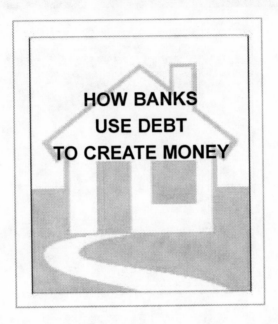

**HOW BANKS
USE DEBT
TO CREATE MONEY**

W hat would you say if I told you that a four-letter word stands between you and financial freedom? Believe it or not, the word is "debt." Consumer education teaches us that "debt" has all of the connotations of a four-letter word.

If you have any doubt that Monopoly is a game with two sets of rules, look carefully at the rules on mortgages. From a money perspective, these rules bring into sharp focus the difference between "Money Limits" and "No Money Limits."

In Monopoly, a mortgage is a desperation strategy. It is the consequence of Monopoly's requirement that you buy with your own money. If you own property and need money, the only way to get money is to take out a mortgage. But to get the mortgage, you have to sell your houses and hotels. Notice that you have to sell them to the Bank at a 50% loss. Then you can get a mortgage for 50% of the value of the property. Ouch!

Let's go back to the Mediterranean Avenue example. If you own Mediterranean Avenue, you spent $60 to buy it. If you mortgage the property, you get only $30 from the Bank. This is consistent with mortgage rates before the changes in FHA mortgage lending in 1934. And to make sure that it is even more painful for you, reinforcing the notion that debt is the ultimate dirty word, you can't collect rent on mortgaged property. So after taking out a mortgage, you can't even collect your measly $2.00 rent.

What happens when you pay off the mortgage, or in Monopoly terminology, you "lift the mortgage"? You have to pay 10% interest on the mortgage. For Mediterranean Avenue, that is $3.00. So, you have in effect paid $33 to get $30. The cost of money is 110% of the purchase price.

Now, let's look how much the Banker profits from your mortgage. Your $33 loss is the Bank's $33 gain. Good for the Bank. Very bad for you.

This is called teaching with a two-by-four. You learn that taking out a mortgage on a property is bad, bad, bad.

The Double Standard About Debt

With the rules on mortgages, we come to the great double standard of our economic system concerning debt. Consumers pay a high price for being in debt. In contrast, the economic system is much kinder to anyone who uses borrowed money to create more money. It comes back to the difference between creating money and using money.

It is also part of the inherent problem of playing Monopoly to learn about real estate investing. It treats debt on rental property as consumer debt rather than investor debt. In every way, the money rules of the Players are rules for consumers rather than investors.

What is the difference between "consumers" and "investors?" If we take the word literally, a consumer "eats up" money. Here's an example: As a consumer, you spend $999.99 for a refrigerator. This means you trade $999.99 for an object. You now have a refrigerator, but you no longer have $999.99 available for use as money. You have converted the energy of the money into a tangible object, the refrigerator. *no other return on the money*

The money is not even potential energy, the way the equity in your home is potential money. As long as you use the refrigerator to store your food, you cannot turn the refrigerator back into money.

You have consumed the money and taken it out of the money supply. This is why the economic system is so hard on consumers. You buy a refrigerator and the refrigerator is not going to make any more money.

In contrast, investors commit money to make a profit. This is why you could buy the same refrigerator and put it into a rental property. That refrigerator becomes an investment because you are using it to make money.

This is why the rules for borrowing are much friendlier for investors than they are for consumers. **When you invest borrowed money, you intend to increase the money supply. When you consume money, you decrease the money supply.**

The difference between borrowing as a consumer and borrowing as an investor is the real issue. And this is also why it's wise to separate the idea of financial freedom from the goal of being debt free. **The real question is: Are you using debt as a consumer or as an investor?**

In the consciousness-raising era of the sixties, people talked about "blowing your mind." It's time to do a bit of mind-blowing and expand our vision far beyond the confines of this little game, which reduces the complexity of money and economic systems to a little cardboard square.

Monopoly teaches you to think small. You can see the game played out in front of you. But you cannot see the bigger picture. In reality, buying and selling real estate occurs in the context of a complex economic system.

I don't pretend to understand very much about the economic system, but I know enough to realize how much Monopoly teaches a fundamental misunderstanding of money. Unlike Monopoly, the amount of money in the money system is constantly in flux, controlled by forces that most of us have no idea exist.

And I also know that financial freedom is not equivalent to freedom from debt. The advice to consumers to pay off all debt makes sense for consumers, but completely misunderstands the role of debt in creating wealth for investors.

If every single person suddenly became debt free, the entire economic system would collapse and we would all go back to living as hunter/gatherers.

At this point, a bit of economic history might help. At the earliest level of human economic development, people lived on a subsistence level, as hunter/gatherers. Over time, human beings began to plant crops.

Agriculture produced a new development in human history. People grew more food than they could eat. As soon as they had a surplus of food, they could trade that food for other items. The surplus of food turned into a surplus of money. And as soon as there was an economic surplus, the society began to divide into social classes based on how much of the surplus people had. Some people had more and some people had less.

Wealth is like cream in milk. It rises to the top. As economic systems grew more complex, developing through stages from hunter/gatherers, to horticultural societies, to agrarian societies, a handful of people controlled most of the economic surplus. That meant that 1-3% of the population owned 80% of the wealth.

What is most interesting is that the same kind of economic division continued into industrial societies and persists in capitalist economies. In the United States, a handful of extremely rich families still controls most of the wealth. It is the same throughout the world. A few people control most of the wealth in almost every economy on planet Earth.

Debt Builds Wealth

Because of this concentration of wealth in the hands of a few, our economic system is built on debt. The extremely wealthy have money to lend. The rest of us borrow their money. The banks, the financial markets, and the bond markets are part of an entire system of intermediaries using the borrowed money of the extremely rich to expand the economy.

Our entire economic system is a debt system. Debt is what makes money. Debt is what increases money. Debt is the mechanism that allows us to increase our living standard.

It's even more complicated than this. The modern debt economy in the United States and every other economic system that has evolved beyond a subsistence economy, is a dance between the extremely rich, financial markets, political systems, and banking systems, played out on the world stage. The money dance is so complicated that it even includes the foreign currency markets, where the world's biggest banks buy and sell currencies, causing the value of currencies to fluctuate. It includes trade deficits and national debts.

In the United States, the Fed is the central bank, which controls the amount of money in the economic system. The Fed is a shadowy institution, formerly called the Federal Reserve. The Fed is a strange hybrid of private banks with federal authority, but not really under government control. It operates mostly out of sight, to keep the money flowing between the extremely rich, the financial markets, the banks, and the consumers, all the while responding to political pressures, both nationally and internationally, and demands by the extremely rich to increase their wealth even more. It holds its meetings in private, making decisions that affect the economic well-being of all of us.

The Fed has the power to increase or decrease the amount of money available in the economic system. They can do this by raising and lowering interest rates.

Have you ever seen a system of locks, such as the locks at the Panama Canal? The Panama Canal is not simply a channel dug across the narrow strip of land between two oceans. It is a hydraulic system to raise or lower the level of water to transport boats through the locks from one body of water to the other.

The boat enters the first lock. A system of hydraulics pumps water into or out of the lock and raises or lowers the level of the boat to the water level of the next lock. The boat enters the next lock. The system increases or decreases the amount of water in that lock. The system carries the boat from one body of water to the next by a series of gradual steps.

This is what the Fed does with money. It raises and lowers the amount of money in the system by raising and lowering interest rates. If there is too much money, there is inflation. If there is not enough money, there is recession.

When the Fed wants to increase the money in the money supply, it lowers the interest rates the commercial banks pay for borrowing money. When it wants to decrease the amount of money, it raises interest rates the commercial banks must pay. When there is too much money, the Fed begins to increase interest rates. This shrinks the amount of money in the system, and the shrinkage continues down to the amount of money available for you to borrow for your mortgage.

This is why everyone listens so carefully when the chairman of the Fed speaks. And this is why raising or lowering interest rates a quarter of a percentage point is such a big deal.

Now this is where you can really see how banks create money. Let's say that the Fed pumps a billion dollars into the economy through the commercial banks. The commercial banks do what banks do. They loan out that money. By the time the commercial banks get through loaning the billion dollars, the commercial banks have created more money. Let's say, five billion. And the commercial banks loan out the five billion to the "thrifts," which are the savings banks, savings and loan banks, corporate banks, and credit unions. The thrifts take those five billion dollars and make loans, creating who knows how many more billion dollars.

Now imagine what would happen if every one suddenly became debt free. The entire economic system would collapse. The lifeblood of the economy is borrowed money. Governments depend on borrowed money. Businesses depend on borrowed money. Consumers depend on borrowed money. And with borrowed money, investors can create more money. Debt is the mechanism that has allowed substantial numbers of real estate investors to make fortunes in the real estate market, especially in recent years.

Monopoly teaches a fundamental misunderstanding of the role of debt in our economic system. The Monopoly winner and the Bank continue to take money out of circulation, until there is not enough left for the game to continue.

If the handful of extremely rich people did what the Monopoly winner does, which is to gather almost all of the money in circulation and hang onto it, the result would be the collapse of our economic system.

Meanwhile, in this economic system built on borrowed money, banks apply a double standard about consumer debt. When you apply to the bank for a mortgage, debt is a liability. The bank will evaluate your credit history and debt-to-income ratio. Every inquiry into your credit score will lower your score. The ideal consumer candidate for a mortgage is some-one who is debt free, with excellent credit history.

At the same time the banker wants you to be debt free, the banker is loaning you borrowed money. The bank is taking deposits from its customers and loaning that money to other customers. This is the heart of the banker's ability to create money. It uses "other people's money" (OPM) to make money.

Investors who understand what the banks understand about money know that the fastest way to create wealth is to leverage debt. What is leverage? Archimedes said, "Give me a lever long enough and I can move the world." A lever allows you to move something you could not do on your own.

The advantage of using leverage in real estate is that you can use a small amount of your own money and end up controlling the whole property. Leverage allows you to buy a property with a little or no money of your own. In fact one of the reasons that people create financial independence through real estate is that they can leverage other people's money (OPM).

For an investor, debt can be your best friend. A mortgage on a property is a specific kind of debt. And this mortgage debt is one of the most powerful examples of using other people's money to buy property you could not afford to buy with your own money.

Compare two strategies for buying rental real estate. In the first strategy, you decide that financial freedom means being debt free. You have a mortgage but want to own the property free and clear. You pump all of your rental profits into the property. Eventually, you own the property. Now you have 100% equity in the property. But you cannot use that money unless you borrow against it or sell the property.

Compare this strategy to own the property debt free with the strategy of taking the profits from your rental property and applying the profits to another property. As long as you can pay the mortgage and the rest of the expenses, you are using the cash flow on the first property to buy another rental property. With the cash flow from that property, you can repeat the process with another rental property.

In the first example, you can pay off the mortgage on one rental property. In the second example, in the same amount of time, you can buy several other rental properties. This is using money the way bankers use money, to keep it moving to create more money.

Let's return once again to the difference between being "Money Limits Investors" and "No Money Limits Investors," especially concerning debt. "Money Limits Investors" who insist on being debt free must use their own money for all of their investing.

In a debt economy, this is something like insisting on not breathing in oxygen because you want to be self-sufficient. It prevents you from using the most powerful wealth building tool available.

"No Money Limits Investors" know the banker's debt secret. Investor debt increases the amount of money you have available for investing. The right kind of debt can be your best friend.

Earlier, I referred to the hologram, which contains the information of the whole from a single perspective. Monopoly is not a hologram of the economic system of the 21st century. It isn't even a hologram of the economic system of the Great Depression. The game of Monopoly is something like the fleas on a dog forming a society and deciding that one is king, without ever recognizing that they are living on a dog.

The Monopoly world view is too small, without recognizing that the money system is so much bigger. The economic system is a debt system, which uses borrowed money to create more money. The real hologram of the economic system begins when you realize that you can use investor debt to create wealth.

In Part I, we looked the difference between "No Money Limits" and "Money Limits." In Part II, we looked at specific elements of the Monopoly game and real estate investing: buying and selling real estate; cash flow; debt. In Part III, we look at the difference a "No Money Limits" perspective can make in our money relationships with buyers, sellers, tenants and especially in ourselves.

PART III

Chapter 10

"NO MONEY LIMITS" COOPERATION

The rules of Monopoly allow only one winner of the game. If only one person can win, all of the other players must lose. And this brings us to the next problem with the Monopoly game as a model for real estate investing. The game requires players to compete with each other for a limited amount of real estate and money.

This zero sum competitive game reflects the economic realities of the Great Depression. While thousands stood in breadlines, a handful made fortunes. For one player to win, the others must lose.

And once again, this rule comes back to the limited money supply. The fundamental belief behind Monopoly is lack of money. Since the money supply cannot increase, the players can win only by taking money from other players. Your goal is to force the other players out of the game.

Private Transactions

The Bank controls the money and controls almost every money trade in the game. However, the rules of Monopoly allow three types of private transactions between Players that are not controlled by the Bank.

- A Player can sell the "Get Out of Jail Free" card to another Player.

- A Player can sell unimproved properties directly to another Player.

- A Player can sell mortgaged property to another Player.

These three exceptions are especially interesting.

They break the pattern of having the Bank in the middle of all money exchanges and point in the direction of private money transactions that bypass the Bank.

They are the only true transactions in the Monopoly game, where almost all money exchanges are trades rather than transactions. Since the prices are not set, the Players can negotiate. These transactions allow the possibility that a Player can actually "make" more money than the face value of the property.

They don't apply to properties with buildings, and so these private arrangements don't involve the primary game of collecting rents on improved properties.

Despite these exceptions, Monopoly is a game won or lost by rents on properties with buildings. Monopoly is a highly competitive trading game with no true transactions concerning improved properties.

These rules also make clear that Monopoly prohibits money partnerships. This is evident from the rule prohibiting money loans between Players. Since Players are not allowed to borrow or lend money to other Players, Players must win or lose with their own money.

The only way to interact with the other players is to buy properties and collect rents from the other players or to pay rent to them.

The psychological effect of playing this highly competitive game is that you are an isolated player doing whatever you can to force the other players to go bankrupt. The last thing you want to do is to help someone else stay in the game because that person might go on to drive you out of the game.

The belief that success means competition reinforces a whole array of social models and beliefs about the "survival of the fittest" and the "law of the jungle" where only the strong prevail. You can see the same belief behind the American mythology of the self-made man who pulls himself up by his bootstraps.

Even Abraham Maslow's "Hierarchy of Needs" is a model of individuals striving to succeed on their own, independently of others. Maslow used the image of a pyramid. The goal of the self-actualized person is to progress upwards to reach the pinnacle of the pyramid. According to the model, only 2% of the population ever reaches this lofty status of being "self-actualized." Although Maslow's "Hierarchy of Needs" has many critics who say that real success involves collaboration and cooperation, success literature often accepts the theory at face value as an accurate description of success. Maslow's model reinforces the belief that success is a solitary quest by an individual.

Whether the image is of pulling yourself up by your bootstraps, climbing the pyramid of the hierarchy of needs, or scaling the ladder of success, we have all learned that success goes to the individual who wins the competition.

This kind of imagery is deeply embedded in our consciousness about what it takes to make money and what it takes to succeed in business. Monopoly simply reinforces the fundamental belief that the road to success is paved with the bodies of your competitors.

As a success model, what is the effect of a game based on competition for a limited money supply? You don't have to look any further than the statistic that 96% of the population will reach 65 without enough money to be financially self-sufficient. Instead of congratulating the 4% who somehow manage to create financial freedom for themselves in this economic system, we all need to ask: "What is wrong with the game? Why do so many lose?"

The short answer is that our economic models teach competition for limited resources as the foundation of wealth. The model itself demands that almost everyone must end the game broke.

What happens when you attempt to create wealth as a real estate investor according to the Monopoly model? It's a highly competitive game and a lonely struggle. You use your own money and do it alone. In other words, you become a "Money Limits Investor."

Will you succeed? Maybe. You might be one of the lucky few who manage to do it all yourself. More likely, you will end up as one of the casualties of those who tried to get started in real estate investing but never made enough money to succeed.

Abundance Is A Team Sport

In contrast to the competitive nature of Monopoly, the fundamental principle of "No Money Limits" investing is that

abundance is a team sport. You can hear this new game in the language of "win-win" instead of "winner-take-all." The more you help others win, the greater the opportunity for you to win.

Let's go back to the physics behind cooperation. At the subatomic structure of reality, quantum physics demonstrates cooperation rather than competition as the most basic model of reality.

As early as the ancient Greeks, science and philosophy identified the atom as the smallest unit of matter that could not be divided. Then physicists discovered subatomic particles—the electrons, protons, and neutrons—thinking they had finally reached the smallest units of matter. Then they discovered even smaller particles. Now physicists identify 12 smaller particles, divided into two classes called leptons and quarks.

The particle that is especially relevant as a model of cooperation rather than competition is the quark. What is absolutely fascinating about the quark is that the quark never exists as a single entity. A quark is always in relationship with two other quarks. Depending on the particular types of quarks involved, these threesomes create either neutrons or protons.

This little excursion into quantum physics demonstrates that the very foundation of reality is relationship rather than the oneness of the atom. In addition, social scientists dispute the notion that competition is the foundation of societies. They identify cooperation as a much more basic social model.

So what does any of this have to do with investing? Let's put this in financial terms. **From a "No Money Limits" perspective, it means that the more you can become involved with partnerships and joint ventures, the more money you will make.**

Look at what happens in Monopoly. Yes, one person wins. One person gets most of the money, but the winner cannot make any more money. The winner-take-all model of Monopoly restricts the amount of money available, even to the winner.

By taking everyone else out of the game, there is no possibility for joint venture relationships to increase the money supply. In Monopoly the winner takes the biggest portion of the pie, but the pie itself cannot get bigger. The only way for the pie to get bigger is to create a game where more people create more money.

The most successful real estate investors understand that investing is a team sport. In fact, most real estate gurus encourage students to build a "team." The team includes real estate appraisers, realtors, bankers, mortgage brokers, bankers, hard money lenders, title companies, contractors, CPAs, and attorneys. All of these related professionals are valuable members of your real estate investing team. The essential point I want to make is these are not your direct competitors.

As long as your team consists of people in related professions, you have not taken the "No Money Limits Investor" step of forming your own quark-type relationship with people who are also investors. Instead of treating other investors as competitors, you find ways to cooperate with them.

What happens to money when you cooperate with others rather than compete with them? The most basic result is that more transactions lead to more money. Cooperation is the fastest way to increase the amount of money in the game.

Cooperation will allow you to buy property you could not afford on your own because you have more money available. Cooperation will allow you to set up all kinds of cooperative agreements.

Real estate investors talk about "bird dogs." A bird dog is somebody who finds a property and passes the information to someone who can buy it. The bird dog makes money by finding properties, not by buying them.

You can also make money as the deal maker. You can be the person who puts together the seller and the person with the money and arranges the deal.

You can also be the one who puts up the money. A bird dog or deal maker can bring a deal to you, and you can be the one to buy if you have money to invest.

There can be joint ventures with putting up capital to buy properties. You can do the work and someone else puts up the money. You can share equity. You can pass off deals when you are not able to make money with them.

Quark's work Together and grow Faster

The point is that there are many different roles you can play when you realize that you will make much more money as a quark than an atom. Or to change the metaphor, you will make more money turning competitors ✕ into partners than you will by attempting to eliminate your competition and win alone. The problem with that model is that your competitors are trying to do the same to you. And since there are more of them than there are of you, you are much more likely to lose than you are to win.

Monopoly and "Money Limits Investors" believe that money is a commodity in limited supply. The key concept behind "No Money Limits" investing is that money is unlimited when you learn the Banker's secret "uncovered and left in sight" that money is made is transactions.

Be a Banker create Money

You Don't Need The Bank For Money

Monopoly teaches you that control of money lies outside of you and it's up to someone else to decide whether or not you are worthy to borrow money. Banks teach you to be powerless about money. You cannot create financial freedom by giving up control of your money to intermediaries. And going through banks reinforces the idea that you have to follow the bank's rules to get money. When you realize that money is created in transactions, you also realize that you do not need the bank.

A significant "No Money Limits Investor" secret is that banks are one source of money but they are not the only source of money.

There is also a whole world of investment money available through private money lenders. Private money lenders can be anyone with some money to invest in real estate. You can borrow from family members, neighbors, friends, and work associates. You can also borrow from "hard money" lenders. All of these options are ways to bypass the bank. If you think that your only option is to borrow from the bank, you are operating with a Monopoly money mindset that the bank controls the money.

Private money transactions can take any form the two parties agree upon. You can set up flexible terms, payments, and rates, usually within less time and with less paperwork than you need to borrow from the bank.

Professional private money lenders, the "hard money" lenders, tend to charge higher interest rates than banks. Why would anyone use hard money when bank mortgages are available? One reason is that private money lenders can move more quickly than banks in approving loans. Another reason is that buying through a bank usually means that you have to qualify for the money. Hard money lenders tend to qualify the property without qualifying you as the borrower.

At the same time, the bank can be the best source of money for investors. Banks tend to have lower interest rates than hard money lenders. Banks can also provide lines of credit, which are especially valuable sources of cash for investing. Banks can be valuable sources for investment money, as long as you are dealing with the bank from a position of power and choice.

When you play your own money game as a "No Money Limits Investor," you realize that you do not need the bank to make money. You have other options, including becoming your own bank.

The quantum reality of financial freedom is that you are in control of your own money game. When you play the Monopoly money game, you depend on others for your money. Money comes from outside of you, after others determine your worthiness to receive it. Asking banks for money reinforces the idea that you are powerless to create money on your own. When you play by "No Money Limits" rules, you realize that you have much more flexibility and many more choices to create and control your own money.

As a model for creating wealth, Monopoly is stuck in the mindset and money beliefs of the Great Depression. In the Monopoly game, the winner amasses money but does nothing to create money through transactions.

The Great Depression ended more than sixty years ago. It's time for a new game with a new understanding of money. Mr. Monopoly had it wrong when he thought that winning meant driving competitors out of business. Yes, I know. The investing world is still full of people doing whatever they can to destroy their competition. And sometimes the worst people seem to win.

When you take off the Depression era Mr. Monopoly glasses, you can see a new vision of money and real estate investing. Money is not currency. Money is an idea, and the only limits to money are the limits of your vision. With this vision, you'll see that you will make more money in joint ventures with others than you will by competing against them.

Chapter 11

A "NO MONEY LIMITS" VISION

The Only Limit To Money Is The Belief That Money Is Limited.

This book is my effort to answer a question: Why do so many people attend real estate seminars, full of hope with the promise of creating financial freedom by investing in real estate, but never succeed?

What is missing? Are people lazy? Do they need more techniques? Are they afraid of success? Afraid of failure? Is there really some "mystery of the mind" that keeps people from success? You can make a case for any of these explanations, and you might be right.

My own answer is that the real obstacle for many potential investors is not a mystery of the mind but a conflict of the heart. This conflict comes from the belief that making money means taking money away from other people.

Motivational speakers often talk about having a strong enough "why." You need to know "why" you want to succeed. They claim that if your "why" is compelling enough, it will motivate you to take the actions necessary for success. They instruct you to imagine what money will bring you. They ask you to visualize the cars, the houses, the boats, and the other trappings of wealth. But for many people, these objects are not a sufficient "why." They are motivated by something stronger than any desire for having the "things" that money can buy.

The "Why Not" Of Success

For people stopped by a conflict of the heart about money, the "why not" of success is often much stronger than any "why" of success. This is especially true in real estate investing.

Many of the techniques of real estate investing, as taught by highly successful real estate gurus, require investors to violate some of their most deeply held values. These techniques teach investors to make a profit from someone else's distress.

I don't think that most real estate gurus intend to teach this message. I personally have never heard a real estate guru teach predatory practices to take advantage of distressed sellers. In fact, I have heard several talk about finding ways to solve the problems of distressed sellers who have no other option. I have been impressed by what I perceived as a genuine desire to do the right thing.

Despite such good intentions, many of the methods taught in real estate seminars require investors to buy properties below market value, to profit when people lose their properties through foreclosure, to obtain properties from people who are over their heads financially. Whatever the motivation of the real estate investor, from the perspective of the distressed home owner, these techniques are Monopoly techniques. You make money by taking advantage of someone else's money crisis.

Obviously, not everyone is bothered by such concerns. Many people feel no qualms about taking advantage of people in financial trouble. I don't imagine that they are reading this book.

My book is for the people who are profoundly bothered by the belief that making money means taking money from other people. And this is why I have used the Monopoly game to focus attention on the money assumptions that keep tenderhearted people struggling with money.

Monopoly makes no pretense about the purpose of the game. It is a game designed to create a winner by taking money away from the rest of the players. It is designed to do what some sensitive people do not want to do. It teaches you to win by causing others to go broke.

The precursor to Monopoly was the "Landlord Game." In 1904, Lizzie Magie created the game as a protest against landlords who drove tenants into poverty through high rents.

In the Great Depression, Charles B. Darrow found the Landlord Game and turned it upside down. Monopoly became a game that celebrated what Magie intended to condemn. Monopoly is a game that teaches landlords to drive their tenants into bankruptcy.

More than sixty years later, people still love Monopoly, while the Landlord Game died an obscure death long ago.

If money is not a problem for you, and you enjoy playing Monopoly, I have no intention of urging you to stop. However, if you struggle with lack of money, if you can't get your real estate investing career off the ground, if you have nagging thoughts that real estate investors are nothing better than sharks in the water looking for blood, then I suggest that the game itself might be part of the problem for you. You might consider if playing Monopoly is really helping you create the necessary mindset and skills to succeed as a real estate investor.

My intention is to get to the roots of the "Money Limits" assumptions that lead to conflicts about creating money, especially through real estate investing. I can think of no better example of these "Money Limits" assumptions than this Depression era game.

From my experience as a teacher, I have observed again and again that the real obstacles to success come in the form of unexamined assumptions. I have seen it so often that I even gave my observation a name. I call it "Kalinda's First Law of the Universe." The law states: **"If you are stuck, you are making an assumption that is keeping you stuck."** While the name is tongue-in-cheek, the reality behind the name is not.

When it comes to making money in real estate, the Monopoly assumption that the way to create wealth is to take money from others is the assumption that keeps people struggling. This assumption is based on the belief that money is a commodity in limited supply. There is only so much to go around. For you to get more, you have to take it away from others.

For many people, especially those raised in religious traditions that teach that "love of money is the root of evil," money itself is the problem. Wanting money is a sign of sinfulness and being rich puts you on the side of evil.

What happens when such people think that they would like to create financial freedom through real estate investing? They come headfirst into a situation requiring them to violate these beliefs about money. They attend real estate seminars and hear that the best way to make money is to find people in financial distress and buy their properties below market value. Consciously or unconsciously, money-conflicted people decide that it's better to fail at real estate investing than become a rich person who profits from others' losses.

Maybe you didn't get this kind of religious teaching, but you did hear that "money doesn't grow on trees." You learned that "you have to make do." You learned that "rich people are selfish and greedy." You learned that "money can't buy happiness." These assumptions about money are deeply rooted in our society. These and a hundred other beliefs about money and rich people leave many of us with deep conflicts about wanting money, especially when it means making money at the expense of other people in distress.

The truth is, most of what any of us learned about money from our families, our religious traditions, schools, and the society in general is enough to keep many of us floundering and struggling for money. Mostly we learned that there is not enough money to go around, and the rich get richer and the poor get poorer. In short, what most of us learned about money is what Monopoly teaches.

Yes, I know it is only a game. But games are powerful teachers, because players become so fully involved emotionally, physically, and intellectually in the game. Every game involves foundational principles. The foundational principle of Monopoly is that money is in short supply and the way to win is to take money from others.

The belief that making money requires hurting other people is based on a misunderstanding of money. Money is energy. When money is no longer imagined as equivalent to currency,

there is no potential limit to money. As long as money remains moving, it can create more money.

Monopoly Misrepresents Money

This is the point on which Monopoly does the greatest harm. Monopoly misrepresents money. In fact, what Monopoly teaches about money and real estate is simply not true. Monopoly is a trading game with almost no capacity to increase the money supply. This violates the process by which money is created. Real estate transactions and mortgages on real estate are two prime examples of the way money is created in our debt economy.

I am not a naïve person. Believe me when I tell you that I know what it is to live in a kind of hell on earth of cruelty and meanness, and to know what it is to do without money. I know what it is to be hungry and dirty, suffering from cold in an unheated house, badly dressed with ripped clothing and shoes with flapping soles, constantly in pain with a mouthful of decayed teeth from lack of dental care. I know what it is to live a life shaped by "Money Limits."

What motivates me is not some kind of pie in the sky attitude that ignores this reality. What really motivates me is the understanding that much of the suffering was unnecessary. So much of the hellishness was related to lack of money and the beliefs of parents who grew up "doing without" in the Great Depression.

I see in Monopoly the money belief that perpetuates misery for so many people. It comes back to the idea that there is simply not enough money to go around. And the only way to win is to cause others to lose.

So many of the techniques in real estate seminars have been used in ways that make life worse for people in distress, with predatory practices such as equity stripping. Even now, various legislative bodies are enacting laws to prevent such investing abuses.

How do you deal fairly with the people whose property you buy, with the tenants who rent from you, with the people who buy your investment properties?

What do you do, if you genuinely want to do the right thing in the world, and hear that the way to make money is to find a seller in distress and buy the property below market value?

As a practical matter, you will find that some people are in distress because they have made a botch of their lives. It's really important to make sure that you don't take on other people's problems and make them your own. And it's equally important that you don't use your real estate business to offer charity to people who cannot or will not take responsibility for their money problems.

I also know horror stories of tenants who have destroyed rental properties because they felt no obligation to take care of them. And for them too, it probably comes back to money. They don't think it is fair that the "rich" landlord has what they don't have. And so they destroy the landlord's property out of spite and jealousy.

The challenge is to draw the line between dealing ethically and honestly with buyers, sellers, and tenants, and also remembering that you are in business. You are not a savior. You are a real estate investor.

And so this brings us to the deeper question of "why"? Why would you want to make money in real estate?

For people with a conflict of the heart about money, the solution is to go beyond any visions of fancy toys and big houses and the rest of the "stuff" that money can buy. The solution is to have a bigger vision of what money can do.

Monopoly cannot teach you to imagine beyond the money limits of its little cardboard square, with its Depression era competitive vision of a world without enough money, where the only way to win is to cause everyone else to lose.

The No Money Limits Game

There is a much better game than Monopoly. It is called "No Money Limits." When you grasp the profound truth that the only limit to money is the belief that money is limited, you realize that you can use money to make life better for yourself and others.

The first result of such a vision is that you can create a life of financial freedom for yourself and the people you love. When you learn the banker's secret uncovered and left in sight, you discover that real estate is one of the most reliable and fastest routes to create money, whenever you need it.

It is similar to the old cliché about learning to fish. If all you have is the fish, you have only a limited amount of food. But when you learn to fish, you have a skill you can use for lifetime.

Learning to make money as a real estate investor is such a skill. When you need money, you can make money. This is real security, based on your knowledge and your skill and your beliefs, rather than hope that you will have enough money to last a lifetime.

You can also use your knowledge and skill to create money to make life better for other people living with money limits. As a real estate investor, with the knowledge of how to make money, you can solve problems for people in trouble in ways that are fair and just.

One of the most limiting of all the money beliefs is that spiritual people should not care about money. In reality, money is simply energy. It is a tool, which can be used for any purpose you intend. It is too powerful a tool to leave in the hands of people who do not care about the wellbeing of others. Money is the lifeblood of our economic system. When you know how to create money, you can liberate yourself and others from the tyranny of living without enough money.

Beyond making money as a real estate investor, when you grasp that money is limited only by vision, you can also envision making a

real difference in the world. **Money is not the answer for every problem, but it goes a long way toward solving many human problems.**

Finally, I return to the place I began, with Napoleon Hill's secret "uncovered and left in sight." I have always found Napoleon Hill's decision to keep his secret hidden a bit annoying and elitist. Maybe it does mean more when it is discovered than when it is revealed. But I am not convinced. Why keep such a liberating insight hidden, when revealing it can make such a difference in people's lives?

I close with a story about an event at a wilderness camp in the Canadian Rockies. About twenty of us were blindfolded and led to a maze in the woods. The maze was laid out with ropes strung together, from tree to tree. The terrain was uneven, with bumps and hollows in the ground. The ropes ranged from a foot to three or four feet off the ground. Our objective was to ring a bell somewhere in the course.

I know that I retraced my steps more than once, coming to a place where the ropes met at a forty-five degree angle, or where a rope ended at a tree. I knew I had come to that same corner before, touched that same tree before. Then I would turn around and go back, trying to find my way without being able to see. Throughout the course, I met others, our hands touching on the ropes as we groped in darkness along the rope maze.

Meanwhile, I could hear the bell ring at least three times. That meant at least three of the participants managed to find their way.

Once, I could tell that I was close to the bell, but I never managed to find my way out of the maze before the time was up. I didn't find the bell. Most of us didn't.

I do know that I persevered. I didn't give up. I kept trying to find my way, back and forth and up and down along the ropes, but I couldn't find my way with my eyes covered.

After we took off our blindfolds, the bell was clear enough. With the blindfolds, most of us couldn't find it.

Vision changes everything. It's the same with the secret "uncovered and left in sight" in Monopoly. With money limits blindfolds on, most of us simply can't see the secret. We stumble along trying to find our way. Some succeed. Most fail.

Going through life with money limits blocks vision just as surely as the blindfold around my eyes blocked my vision in the rope maze.

But now, your blindfolds are off. You can see beyond the limited money vision of the little cardboard square with its familiar names of Mediterranean Avenue, St. Charles Place, and Boardwalk. What vision could you have for your life if you could see beyond the "Money Limits" that have kept you stumbling through the money maze?

You can now see the secret "uncovered and left in sight." **The question is: What are you going to do with your new vision of quantum possibilities as a "No Money Limits Investor?"**

K alinda Rose Stevenson, founder of Debt or Alive, Inc, is an academic turned entrepreneur. Through her own transition from former Adjunct Professor and Lecturer at various schools of the Graduate Theological Union in Berkeley, CA, to online marketer, certified Guerrilla Marketing Coach, author of ebooks and online articles, and real estate investor, she is committed to teaching others what she learned the hard way about living life with No Money Limits (www.nomoneylimits.com). Her weekly online newsletter, "Abundantly Alive Now!" (www.abundantlyalivenow.com) has subscribers on six continents. She lives in the San Francisco Bay Area.

FREE AUDIO BONUS

FREE Audio Recording
By
KALINDA ROSE STEVENSON, PH.D.

"HOW TO GET OUT OF DEBT AND FEEL ABUNDANTLY ALIVE."

Are you struggling with debt? There is a solution for debt, and it is not the solution that you will hear about in debt reduction programs.

The truth is: As along as you focus on "getting out of debt," you will never succeed. The only real solution to debt is to create abundance.

Listen as Kalinda Rose Stevenson reveals the reason why most debt reduction programs cannot work and how you can create abundance in your life.

DOWNLOAD RECORDING AT
http://www.nomoneylimits.com/nmlbookbonus

Printed in the United States
108612LV00009B/31-66/A